That Still, Small Voice

Hearing the Voice of God in the Commonplace

Grace & Peace
Bruce

Rev. Bruce L. Taylor

To Bob and Virginia
(good friends)
Happy Trails,
Suzanne
Aug, 2019

Preface

That Still, Small Voice is an anthology of newsletter reflections I wrote during my 25 years of ministry in the Mississippi Conference of the United Methodist Church. Most were written during the ten plus years I served as the founding pastor of Parkway Hills UMC in Madison, MS, although I did write during my appointments to other churches. At each church I was told by church members and encouraged by friends to write a book. So, I did. And this is it. A collection of those musings on everything from everyday people I've observed to the flora and fauna of God's creation to the grief of losing my parents to the losses and blessings of Hurricane Katrina in August 2005.

While this publication is certainly in response to the requests and encouragement of people through the years, I publish this book with the hope you will be prodded to open yourselves to new, or perhaps forgotten, sensory experiences of the many wonders around us. Wonders we take for granted and have since lost their significance and meaning. Expressions of Divine creativity that have become routine and their wondrous nature diminished. Overlooked opportunities to walk, however briefly, with those persons who cross our paths. We have been gifted with five senses through which we may know the fullness of our time on this earth. However, because of the distractions of this world in which we exist, our preoccupation with the many details of our daily lives, and a spiritual amnesia running rampant in our culture our eyesight has clouded, our ears have become tone-deaf, our sense of smell desensitized, touch indifferent, and taste categorical. Through my experiences chronicled in these reflections it is, again, my hope that you will be stirred to appreciate God's creation with heightened senses and what has become commonplace will become miraculous once again.

While I've not been a practitioner of three-point sermons, there are three primary reasons behind this book. If you're not counting, I've mentioned two. So, thirdly… The same distractions that hinder our ability, or willingness, to embrace the full richness of being also hampers our capacity, or desire, to hear God speak to us through the everyday occurrences that constitute life. In every experience and encounter God's still, small voice speaks to listening hearts and attentive spirits. God's voice affirms and challenges; comforts and disturbs; inspires and encourages. When we hear the voice of God in the commonplace we become increasing aware of God's constant presence in our lives. We are reminded of the promises of

God and assured of God's grace and love which is sufficient for our every need. In these brief reflections, may you also hear God's messages and I hope you will be inspired to pause and reflect long enough to hear God's still, small voice speak to you in the midst of the daily experiences of your life.

In the end, I hope this book brings enjoyment, enlightenment, and inspiration.

Grace and peace,

Rev. Bruce Taylor

Introduction

I've lived all my life close to the earth. As a child, without modern day technology to otherwise entertain me, I spent most of my time outdoors. In the summer my siblings, cousins, neighbors, and I would stay out until dark making up games, catching lightning bugs, doing whatever we could to avoid bath time. During the day, we roamed the woods, explored the fields, waded the creeks, and walked the railroad track that passed through my hometown. Though we had a family dog growing up, my pet menagerie often included snakes, lizards, turtles, a June Bug on a thread, or any other living thing I could catch and keep in a cage, pen, or cigar box. When I walked into the house holding a jar or box my mother would say, "Now, Bruce Lynn, you just keep on walking out the door with that thing. I don't want a snake in my house!" She didn't know if it was a snake or not but that didn't matter. I kept walking.

I don't remember a summer when I didn't have a garden. As a youngster my dad gave me a part of the garden he and my granddaddy tilled. That section was mine to plant, till, keep, and harvest. I remember one of the last things my other granddaddy said before he died was, "Has Bruce planted his garden yet?" A special thought from a special man. One I've never forgotten.

I planted whatever Daddy and Granddaddy planted, and I remember well my parents, grandparents, aunts and uncles tending the garden. Early and late. Watering, hoeing, poisoning, picking. Cleaning, shelling, snapping, cooking, and canning. I came to appreciate early on the wonderful fragrances in the garden: rich earth, green plants, luscious fruits. So even if it were a couple of tomato plants, I don't remember a summer without a garden.

I was an active member of Boy Scout Troop 46 and in 1966 I became an Eagle Scout. Committed parents, a dedicated Scoutmaster, encouraging friends and a faithful church made the rank of Eagle possible. To get there we camped, backpacked, paddled the lakes and streams, and combed the hills and hollows for every item on our scavenger hunt list. I worked two summers on the staff at Camp Binachi, the camp for the Choctaw Area Council. I taught two "courses" to younger scouts – Nature and Reptile Study merit badges. We walked, observed, and collected. Animal tracks, insects, plants, reptiles, amphibians, and whatever mammal may cross our path. Our class site was complete with cages containing a myriad of creatures. One summer we had a cottonmouth moccasin. I don't like cottonmouth moccasins. Sorry. One week that summer there was an assistant troop leader who was a student at a college up in Tennessee. He decided we should milk the venom from the cottonmouth's fangs. I helped. I held its tail, extending my skinny arm as far as the bones and tendons would permit. Like I said, I don't like water moccasins.

In high school and college, I loved science, especially the natural sciences. In zoology a drop of stagnant water under the microscope revealed a world of organisms of shapes and forms that must be the pattern for the creatures of science fiction and horror movies. One of my favorite college courses was botany taught by George Mason. One of the class requirements was a wildflower collection of fifty spring wildflowers - pressed, dried, mounted, and classified. We identified the flowers using microscopes, technical classification books, and photographic comparison. Mr. Mason took us on field trips to give us an opportunity to benefit from his expertise. One of the trips took us to Harris Hill and subsequently along the upper reaches of the Chunky River that meandered through the hills.

On these field trips we located wildflowers that thrived in various habitats from the bogs where springs fed the river to leaf-covered hillsides to the roadsides of dusty country roads to the lawn of our familiar college campus. Henbit. Bluets. Spring Beauties. Jack-in-the-Pulpit. Trilliums of distinctive form and color. Little Brown Jugs with flowers hiding their unique shape beneath the decaying leaves on the hillsides. Here, there, and everywhere were delicate flowers of every color in the spectrum. Each one with structure and detail unique to its specific habitat and its distinctive method of reproduction.

I'll be forever grateful to George Mason for that eye-opening, life-changing, out-of-the-classroom experience. All my life I had been surrounded by such intricate detail and beauty and I hadn't even noticed. So, from that point on, I walked more cautiously and attentively. Now, almost 50 years later, I still do. One annual ritual is the appearance of the bluets. For me, the advent of the bluet marks the arrival of spring as they emerge and bloom in dainty pastel colors on the sun-warmed landscape.

In graduate school I took courses in genetics, biochemistry, and cell biology but the courses I enjoyed the most were, again, in the area of natural science. I had knowledge of many terrestrial insects, reptiles, and amphibians, but graduate courses revealed new hidden wonders. In the organic debris rotting on the pond bottom were the grotesque nymphs of the dragonfly and damselfly. On the underside of rocks in the streams and creeks were the scorpion-like aquatic life stages of the mayfly and stonefly. In leaf packs and beaver dams were the over-sized maggot of the mosquito hawk. Seines dragged through streams and water holes captured fish, mudpuppies, eels, and an occasional snake, gratefully no cottonmouth moccasins. Nets held in the current downstream of a muddled logjam or gravel bar snared brilliantly colored darters and other aquatic creatures the names of which I've since forgotten. All as varied and wondrous as the wildflowers, though perhaps not as beautiful. But, beauty is in the eyes of the beholder.

The splendor of God and the wonders of life are evident all around. Micro and macro. Living and inert. Observed and over-looked. Obvious and obscure. A rainbow hung in the clouds. A walk on a clear, moonless night under a canopy of stars, shadows from the starlight. A farmer standing waist-deep in a cotton field. The coolness and smells of the woodlands after an early morning rain. A dog curled up at your feet or a cat in your lap. Friends and family members who have and will always be a part of your life and people who momentarily cross your path and may never be met again.

Around the time I turned 40, my eyesight changed and reading glasses became essential. A few years later my vision weakened to the point new eye glasses were necessary for me to see clearly and in detail, near and far. Each annual exam resulted in a new prescription to correct my eyesight. Then came the cataract diagnosis and the anticipation for the day my cataracts would be ripe for the harvest. Blurred vision, halos surrounding headlights, dimmed sunlight, and failing night vision became the order of each day. Finally, after years of waiting, my cataracts were declared ready. Just after my 66th birthday, I got new eyes. The natural lenses of my eyes were replaced with man-made lenses. Just like that 20/20 vision. Glasses for reading only. Details at a distance like I hadn't seen in years!

Every minute of every day is an opportunity to perceive our surroundings in a way that each scene becomes a part of a larger picture. Such a perception is possible when we have new eyes to see. Not rose-colored glasses. Not shaded glasses that screen our outlook. Certainly not blinders. But, new eyes. Eyes with which we bask in the brilliant light but also peer into the dark corners. Eyes with which we really see, not just notice. Eyes that not only perceive but interpret. Eyes of the mind. Eyes of the heart. Eyes of the soul.

Seminary education with a focus on the study of Scripture and Theology added a new dimension to the awareness of my surroundings. Through generalized studies of the New and Old Testaments and specialized studies on specific books in the Old and New Testaments, I gained new insights into God's story plus learned the techniques to properly interpret the messages recorded in God's story. Rather than trying to glean the riches of Scripture through simply reading, seminary taught me to dig deeper, search further, and explore new territory.

Bible study became something akin to marine biology. The oceans, from the warm, sunlit surface to the greatest depths enveloped in cold and darkness, are teeming with a diverse population of life. Each organism has adapted to survive in a specific habitat influenced by light and temperature. So as one descends through the depths, one discovers a continuous array of creatures and organisms. Even at the greatest depths where no one would expect life, scientists have discovered a profusion of life forms that thrive in the darkness.

So, I guess we've looped back for moment to those uniquely designed creatures that exist beyond our vision and in some cases even beyond our imagination. The variations of life found at the different depths and numerous habitats in the ocean become a metaphor of the richness of Scripture, the miracle of Scripture. There is a surface message to the readers of the Bible, one that is valid and meaningful. As one not only reads but studies in greater depth the story of God recorded in the Scriptures, new messages come to light. Deeper and deeper studies continue to reveal unforeseen and unexpected messages that speak in the context of the readers' lives. Messages that would never be known otherwise. Messages that rattle the ceiling, shake the foundations. Messages that have the capacity to transform us, to reveal what otherwise can't be seen, to equip us to transform our world. Yet, how many of us, perhaps out of fear, swim only at the surface and never venture to the more challenging depths and the abundant life they offer. Seminary taught me how and challenged me to dive deep. I'm diving in.

I had heard horror stories of Systematic Theology, but the study of Karl Barth, Paul Tillich, James Cone, John Wesley, and others forged a path for me to formulate a personal theology. Christ and Culture and The Meaning of Revelation both by H. Richard Niebuhr were profound in their influence on my evolving theology. While I could identify with elements of each theologian, my personal theology, my personal understanding of the nature of God, grew through study, reflection, conversation, meditation, and prayer. Even mowing the lawn was an opportunity for theological thought and reflection. In fact, it was while mowing one day that I suddenly "saw" what Friedrich Schleiermacher, German theologian and preacher, was saying. Not sure that I totally understood him, but at least got a glimmer into Schleiermacher's theology. Pretty miraculous to me.

The courses at Candler School of Theology at Emory University were both stand-alone and interconnected. All contributed to a tough, inspirational, academic, theological education. To exegete the Scriptures with noted Biblical scholars Fred Craddock, Gene Tucker, Carl Holladay, and John Hayes; to trace the history of Christian thought with Bill Mallard, Roberta Bondi, and Brooks Holifield; to engage in conversation with theologians Don Saliers and Walter Lowe; to study under scholars in their respective fields of expertise conferred to me an exceptional seminary education. Even more, through my relationships with these people of faith I was able to glean elements of their personal understanding of God to consider as a part of my own.

Biblical scholarship intertwined with the pilgrimage of Christian history and conversations with present and past theologians led to the greatest revelation of my seminary experience, perhaps the greatest revelation in my life, the unfathomable love of God. And the product of that love - extravagant grace. As Archbishop Desmond Tutu said to us at graduation, and others have said through various media, "The bad news is there is nothing you can do to make God love you more; the good news is there is nothing you can do to make God love you less." God's love is unconditional, relentless, unceasing, and always at its utmost. God's love is a divine gift. Grace.

My understanding of God's love and God's grace embraced the realization that God's love and God's grace are incomprehensible. The limits of the human mind, intelligence, and imagination prevent us from fully penetrating the mystery and extent of God's love and grace. We can only understand the Divine as far as the parameters of our human mind and human "heart" will permit. The insights into the nature of God are exemplified in God's faithfulness to God's people in the early stories of Genesis, as God calls apart the Hebrew people, when God stays with God's people even when they choose not to stay with him, in God's relentless desire to maintain a relationship despite the people's apostasy, in the fulfillment of promises despite rebellion, in the gift of God's Son to an undeserving world, in the gift of the Holy Spirit at Pentecost and the birth of the Church.

Whereas Jesus Christ was the revelation and presence of God in human flesh in distinct time and place, the Holy Spirit is the continuing revelation and presence of God in all times and all places, the ubiquitous nature of

God. Through the Holy Spirit we experience the pervasive presence of God and, for those so attuned, hear the voice of the God who speaks to us even in the commonplace encounters of our daily lives.

So... take my lifelong love and fascination of the earth and its inhabitants, however small or great, add a healthy dose of Biblical and theological studies, and, for good measure, mix in an obsessive-compulsive personality and you have the recipe for discerning God's message brought to me in the form of hilarity, tragedy, grandeur, simplicity, the extraordinary, and the commonplace. Such I have done over the years of my ministry as I have observed, discovered, witnessed, and personally experienced. Listening carefully for God's message. Sitting in a quiet, comfortable place and writing the words that were circulating in my mind. Now, after many encouraging words from people in my life and after much procrastination, these thoughts, meditations, and reflections are embraced within the covers of this book, *That Still, Small Voice: Hearing the Voice of God in the Commonplace*. I hope they speak to you. Better yet, I pray that this book will inspire you to take the time to hear the voice of God in your own commonplace encounters of life.

That Still, Small Voice

Hearing the Voice of God in the Commonplace

People,
Places,
and
Things

Good Hope

The rock must weigh well over 100 pounds. It was all I could do to lift it onto the bed of my truck. I found the rock just down the hill in the woods. Aware of the apparent weight of the rock I surveyed my options of getting it in my truck a hundred feet away. With the number of trees that stood between me and the truck there wasn't any way I could get the truck closer, pull the rock up the hill, and hoist it in. The only option was to roll the rock through the trees, up the hill, to the truck, one-half turn at a time. Once at the tailgate, with scratched hands and raw fingers, the last 3 feet were the hardest. Vertical. From the ground to the bed. Injuries resulted from decisions like this. My greatest effort lifted the stone just high enough and once positioned and braced, my rock and I headed home. The old sandstone rock now has a place of honor in our flower bed.

I wouldn't go to this much trouble for just any rock. This rock is special. This rock was at one time one of the foundation stones of Good Hope Methodist Church. About 8 miles out in the country from Decatur, in the Beulah Hubbard community, Good Hope United Methodist Church served the people of the rural community. The lapboard, white-washed, one-room church was built back in the mid-1800s on a foundation of large sandstone rocks. Susan's great-grandfather helped build the church. The Johnson place was just down the road. Still is.

Inside, curtains pulled along galvanized steel pipe formed the classrooms. A wood heater warmed the room. In the age of modernization, the wood heater was replaced by two large space heaters connected to a propane tank outside. There was an altar table, pulpit, altar rail, and piano. A cross and an arrangement of plastic flowers sat on the table and a picture of Jesus hung on the wall behind the pulpit. Wooden pews, no cushions, with "Good Hope M. E. Church" scrawled in chalk across the back provided the seating. Women on the preacher's left. Men on the right.

In the later years Good Hope was paired with Decatur Methodist Church to form the Decatur-Good Hope Charge. The Decatur pastor would preach an early service at Good Hope and be back in town in time for the eleven o'clock service. When I first decided to pursue the ordained ministry, the Rev. Hank Winstead was pastor of the Decatur-Good Hope Charge. After being approved by the Charge Conference, Brother Winstead decided Good Hope would be valuable experience for me. It also meant he wouldn't have to go out early. I preached at Good Hope for four years, during and after my college years.

For four years I got up early on Sunday mornings to preach at Good Hope. In those four years Daddy only missed two Sundays that I remember. He and I traveled the dusty (or muddy) dirt roads together. The third companion on the weekly journey was Susan, the pianist. We were dating at the time. If everyone were there, we had 8 in attendance. The preacher's pay was whatever the offering was. Daddy always put in a check for five dollars. The service was the traditional "hymn sandwich" service. Hymn, hymn, scripture, prayer, hymn, etc. The sermon simple, short. I was a college student with no theological education. I still value those four years. With Daddy. With Susan. With the folks of Good Hope Methodist Church - the Glens, the Frinks, the Crawfords – they were the real foundation, not sandstone rocks.

Good Hope Methodist Church is gone now. With the passing of time, death took church members. Others moved to town where there were opportunities for the children. Good Hope ceased as a worshipping congregation. The building still stood for several years on the foundation of sandstone. Despite efforts to maintain it, the building fell into disrepair. Eventually, the Mississippi Conference of the UMC sold the property. The furnishings were distributed for posterity. The building was burned so the community volunteer fire department could practice. The remains were bulldozed, the ground leveled, and the foundation stones covered up or pushed down into the woods. Good Hope Methodist Church was gone.

Today, pine trees and shrubs have taken over and evidence of the church is all but disappeared. All except one large piece of sandstone down the hill in the woods that now rests in my flower bed. A reminder. A reminder that time passes. A reminder that things change. A reminder of that white-washed, lap-board building filled with praise, thanksgiving, Good News, stories. A reminder that the true foundation of the church is not the rocks on which it stands. The true foundation is Jesus Christ and the people who commit themselves to the ministry of Jesus Christ through the church. A reminder that the real strength of the church is found in its people. Like you.

The Gateway Pine

On a shelf in my office there is a beautifully crafted wooden bowl. The smooth outer surface shines with the rich colors of pine. The grains in the wood create fascinating shapes and figures as they wind their way around the circumference of the bowl. Knots provide evidence of limbs attached to the once viable trunk of the pine tree. On the flat, bottom surface the craftsman has written his name, Bob Russell, and the name of the pine from which the bowl is made, "The Gateway Pine."

Back in 1994 when the Parkway Hills UMC property was purchased, we knew we had a treasure. A gently rolling hillside. Heavily forested with grand oaks and magnificent pines. Deer, squirrels, rabbits, egg-laying turtles from a nearby lake. An occasional copperhead stumbled upon while clearing the land for congregational outings. And… one adolescent pine tree bent over, but not broken, by an ice storm in the not-so-distant past.

So beautiful was the land that every measure was taken to preserve the natural splendor and the integrity of the site. A landscape architect, design architect, and contractor were hired to partner with us in the layout, design, and construction of the buildings. The landscape architect surveyed the property, mapped the track of the sun above and direction of the prevailing winds of summer and winter. One of his recommendations was that the youthful pine, already bent from the elements, would not survive and should be removed. As I said, every effort was made to maintain the natural integrity of the site. Bent or straight that pine was a part of the natural integrity. It stayed.

As the site was cleared, as the congregation gathered for picnics, crawfish boils, and Easter sunrise services, as buildings were built, and as asphalt parking lots were laid, the bent-over pine grew. Its trunk arched out parallel to the ground, twelve feet below. The landscape architect, the same who thought it should go, designed the driveway so entering and departing worshippers would pass under that pine. "The Gateway Pine."

Fascinating in its unique shape, it didn't have the grandeur of the 150-foot pines and the 100-year-old oaks. The Gateway Pine survived the onslaught of pine beetles when the great, tall pines met their demise. That "useless, ugly" tree bent, but did not break, in subsequent ice storms as did the enormous oaks. One summer as log trucks were

7

hauling out the remains of pines killed by the beetle invasion, one truck, too tall to pass under The Gateway Pine, caught the arching trunk and twisted it until it cracked. A large, gaping crack split the supporting trunk to the ground. "Should the Gateway Pine remain? It will surely die." "As long as it lives, it will remain."

They said there were other trees that should be removed. Some would die, they said, because there was too much soil covering their roots. Others that would die because of asphalt and sidewalks. Each time our reply, when they die we'll cut them down. Until then.... As long as they live, let them stay.

The Gateway Pine wasn't really good for much. It didn't provide shade for the children. It couldn't be harvested for lumber and construction. It was bent, diseased, cracked. The Gateway Pine didn't fit our usual "criteria" for health, usefulness, value, or worth. It was outside the box. It was unique. It still lived. It was a part of God's creation. Who was I, who are we to make a judgment, a distinction? I/we can see only the surface, not the heart, not the future. I/we see with limited vision, with myopic eyes and an imperfect heart. But, God... As long as something lives, there are possibilities – for change, for betterment, for good. As long as there is life, there are the possibilities of God.

In the end, the weight of the out-reaching arch became too heavy and the cracked and diseased trunk could no longer support the weight. The weakened trunk gave way and The Gateway Pine drooped and rested on the asphalt drive below. The Gateway Pine was no more. But, it went naturally, in its own time, in its own way.

The Gateway Pine lived for over 10 years from the time it was discovered. It grew. It became a unique feature in the landscape of the church. It became, in a sense, a part of the church. It became a symbol of grace.

The Family Up the Road

Last Sunday it was a real big penny. One Sunday it was an alarm clock. Another Sunday a mirror. It's… "The Box." The stimulus for the children's moments. The only rule is that "The Box" does not contain a living creature and, preferably, no dead creatures, either. A feather. A ballet slipper. An egg whisk. You name it. The box has just about had it in it.

One Sunday morning I opened the box to find three pieces of scrap paper. On one piece was written the message, "WHAT GOD WANTS US TO HAVE!" On the second scrap of paper there were six drawings each labeled in all caps: "SHIRT", "PANTS", "COAT", "SHOES", "HAT", and "SOCKS". My heart ached. How would I form a children's sermon around the box on this Sunday? I knew the child. I also knew he and his little brother lacked most of the things on the list. The third shred of paper also contained a simple drawing labeled, "Happy family." Then under each character were the words "father", "mother", and "children." Under childlike sketches of a dog and kitten the word "pets" was simply written. My heart ached even more. I knew that he and his little brother didn't have this either.

The mother was unable to work. The father was in jail on drug charges. They lived just up the road from the church in a house with few conveniences, if any. No transportation. They walked along the road in front of the church to the only store in the community. I remember the boys visiting our house. They played with our son's toys as if they didn't have toys of their own. They didn't. Each Christmas our church adopted the family. Carried them canned food and staple items, maybe a turkey. Paid their utility bills when there was no income. Church members voluntarily picked up the boys and carried them to Sunday school and Vacation Bible School

We don't have to travel very far to find others like this family. Parents who want to provide for their children and give them the things "God wants us to have". Boys and girls who don't have proper clothing for school and the impending winter weather. Babies who don't receive proper medical care. Older adults who can't pay for expensive medicines and treatments. As Christians, we are called to care. As disciples, we are called to respond. As the church, we are called to be the Body of Christ – today – in the world – in our country – in our state – in our locality. Let us hear the call.

9

The Cotton Farmer

He was standing waist-deep in cotton. Acres and acres of cotton plants surrounded him. He gently examined the dark green foliage and closely inspected the yellow blossoms. Out in the distance the corn crop stood, once green, now brown, nearing harvest. As I drove past, I could imagine the farmer's sense of pride. His cotton crop tall and healthy, promising a bumper crop this year. In a few more weeks his corn will be safely in the crib.

Back in the spring after the rains had lessened and the ground had dried, he tilled the soil and formed the rows for planting. His massive machines planted the seeds, filled the soil with nutrients, and sprayed for weeds and pests. Mother Nature provided nourishing rainfall and warm sunshine. Now after weeks and months of waiting, of wondering, he was seeing the fruits of his hard labors. Tall, healthy, green, blooming. If everything goes well in a couple of more months his massive machines will return to the field and bring in the harvest. That is, if everything goes well. If...

At this point there is not much the farmer can do but to sit, watch, and wait. If bugs appear he can spray. If weeds begin to take over he can spray. But, there is too much yet up in the air. There is still much that can happen between now and harvest. There is much that is beyond his control. What if the rains don't stop and his massive machines can't get into the fields for harvest? What if a violent storm strikes and hailstones clobber his healthy plants? What if...? Farmers live with the "what ifs." They know the dangers of the "what ifs." Some quit in the face of the "what ifs." Hang it up. Give up. Sell out. How does anyone face year after year of "what ifs"? It's not worth the risk, not worth the worry, not worth the pain, not worth the loss.

Others hang in there. Stick it out. Start over if need be. They know there are things in this world and in this life beyond their control. Some years are good, some bad. Reap the harvest of the good years, prepare for the bad. "Some days are diamonds," says a John Denver song, "some days are stone." Good days make up for the bad. Good years compensate for the bad. After all, it's those good times; it's those years that are diamonds that farmers long for, work for, live for, that make life worth living.

However, every farmer knows that one of these years, one of these days, the "what ifs" will come, at least one, sometimes more. So, the

10

good farmer does everything possible to prepare for the "what ifs." That's all the farmer can do. "What ifs" will happen. "What ifs" will come. "What ifs" are a part of living in an imperfect world. While the perfect has been shown to us, it is not yet here. "What ifs" are a part of life. They are unavoidable, in most cases, unpreventable, and while the scientific data can be analyzed to determine how the phenomena occur, the philosophical or theological reasons why cannot always be understood. The best explanation? It's life, and in life, "what ifs" come along every day.

So what choices are there? Quit? Hang it up? Give up? Or hang in there. Stick it out. Take the risk. The key to handling the "what ifs" is to prepare for the inevitable and to be as ready as possible. Prepare. Work on defense. The best offense is a good defense? And... have faith. Not that we will get what we want, what we think we deserve, or even what we need. Faith. Not that everything will work out the way we want it or the way we think it should. Faith. Not that everything will go our way or that the "what ifs" will never come. They will. It's life. Faith. Not having all the right answers and accurate explanations and solid theological insights. Faith.... knowing that in spite of what happens, knowing that when the "what ifs" do come, God does not abandon us. The God who has gone before us, goes with us. Faith is knowing that God is at work even in the dark times, the difficult times, the struggles, the pain, the "what ifs." Faith is believing, knowing, that God is still at work, in life's "what ifs" to bring about God's ultimate will. All we have to do is have faith. But all too often faith is something we want on our terms. Faith. Nobody said it was going to be easy.

Bayou Cosotte Redfish

The list from my fishing outings now includes more pinfish, one more of those fish that makes the grunting noise, countless well-fed pinfish that missed the hook, a dollar bill and a rusty pair of pliers. Okay, I didn't actually catch the dollar bill or the pliers. I found the dollar bill floating near the water's edge and I found the pliers in the rocks. The list also now includes two redfish and one speckled trout. Yep, edible fish. Only one made it to my grill.

A couple of folks have figured out my secret fishing hole. That I've actually caught fish there will probably raise a lot more inquiries and maybe a few spies snooping around. For the first few times I fished my secret spot, I was the only one there. Fishing mostly with dead shrimp, I spent a lot of my time feeding the little ones and baiting my hook. Then, on one cast, my cork disappeared beneath the surface in a strong, quick strike. This one was different from all the rest. Not a series of little pecks and a brief submersion of the cork. On this strike, the cork went under and stayed under. Disappeared completely in the depths. I pulled back on my rod to set the hook and the fight was on.

Adrenaline flowed in the heat of the battle. The fish pulled and ran. I adjusted the drag on my reel. Taking no chances on broken line. New at this experience, I didn't know what I had. It could have been a whale for all I knew. I only knew it was no pinfish, no grunting fish, no oyster shell, no dollar bill. I was determined to land the monster.

Once landed, I still didn't know what I had. I only knew I had a fish that had swallowed my hook, I had no pliers (yet), I had no gloves, and no stringer or ice chest. Like a kid with his first fish, which it was, I carried the fish with bleeding hands and swollen pride to a nearby business for identification. Redfish. Twenty-two inches. A keeper. But I had nothing to keep it on.

Unbeknownst to me, a young couple was fishing on a pier not too far from where I was fishing. No sooner had I landed the whopper than I was joined by the young Hispanic man. I don't know who was more excited. He offered suggestions. Bragged for me. Delighted in the experience with me. I have no idea who he was. I didn't even know he was there. It was like he came out of nowhere. I didn't know his name. He didn't know mine. That we were different, there was no doubt. But for one brief instant, despite the absence of formal introductions, in spite of the differences that could have divided us, for one brief moment there was common ground on which we stood. A redfish. Fishing. For one brief moment in time, we were brothers. Maybe we were not as different as we seemed. I cut the line and gave away my first-ever Redfish to a young Hispanic brother I may never see again.

On subsequent trips to my honey hole, I found that my secret spot was no secret at all. On one outing I shared the spot with two African-American men. They caught one White Trout after another. I caught nothing. Fed the little ones, again. But, again, the experience of fishing overcame the obvious differences between us and we found common ground.

On my last fishing trip, I found my spot shared with a small group of African-American and Hispanic fisherpersons. A couple of young children whooping it up when they pulled in a pinfish. Two women who waited patiently for a fish to take their hook. A group of 5 or 6 young men, who fished, laughed, taunted, and generally just enjoyed being together.

Disappointed that I couldn't get to my favorite spot, I settled in as close to the others as I felt comfortable that I was not imposing on their spot. We mainly kept our distance. No talk or chatter between us. I baited with dead shrimp and fed the little ones. Then, on one cast, that tell-tale strike again. The cork disappeared beneath the surface. I set the hook and the fight was on. Before I could get the fish out of the water, I was surrounded by the men from down the shore. I don't know how they got there as fast as they did. I don't know who was more excited. One practically waded in to retrieve the fish lest the fish get away. Another advised me against grabbing with my hands – a lesson I had learned with my first fish. A third held the fish once landed while I cut the line. There was a miraculous camaraderie, a miraculous spirit that prevailed between us from that time forward. I placed the fish on my stringer and in the water under their direction. We chatted back and forth for the remainder of the day. I moved a little closer.

I never knew any of their names. They didn't know mine. We were different, very different, no doubt. But not entirely different. For a few brief moments, we found common ground on which we could stand and celebrate. For a few brief moments in time, we were brothers. For just a little while there was more that united us than divided us. What united us was more important than anything that would divide us. That which united us, in fact, overcame dissimilarities that separated us.

What a wonderful world this would be if each of us spent less time focusing on differences that divide and more time on commonalities that unite. What a wonderful time this would be if each of us spent less time judging others and spent more time searching for common ground on which we can stand and celebrate life together.

Fishing Flashbacks

Late afternoon. Clear skies. South wind. Standing thigh-deep in the waters off the east end of Horn Island. The waves breaking on the beach behind me. Fly rod in hand. Looking down the beach into the setting sun I could see the silhouettes of my fishing partners scouting the waters, fanning the air with their rods to put their fly in just the right spot. At this point in the story, I would add, "It just doesn't get any better than this."

In the parking lot Scott had decided we'd go to Horn Island rather than Petit Bois looking for redfish, trout, or, for me, anything I might fool with my fly. Rick caught a sheepshead and a redfish about the size of your finger. Scott snagged a pinfish in the eye. I caught nothing. But that was alright. It was my first experience salt-water flyfishing and the first time I had set foot on historic Horn Island. Sometimes *catching* fish is just icing on the cake. Also, as someone has said, that's why they call it fishing and not catching.

I have some great fishing memories from those two years at Pascagoula. I fished from Red Creek up river to the oil rigs off shore. Calvin and I fished some of his secret spots above Cumbest Bluff. Flyfishing and casting for bass, we caught a few, but not many. But I saw the beauty of the Pascagoula River system and the most massive cypress trees and stumps I've ever seen in my life. Calvin, Gerri, Ben, Susan, and I then enjoyed fried chicken from KFC. Hey, you have to have a backup plan. Sometimes they bite. Sometimes they don't.

With Johnny I fished for redfish and speckled trout from the Highway 609 bridge to inner harbor. We didn't catch anything that day, but it was still a great day. I saw the beauty of the river and the marshes in a way I would never have seen otherwise and did something I had never done before. Last spring Gene felt sorry for me in my repeatedly failed attempts to catch a flounder. Gene picked me up one day, took me to Beach Park, and showed me how to catch a flounder with bull minnows. I caught two or three that day with Gene. Flounder fishing became a mini escape for me in the afternoons. It's nothing like catching a flounder, taking it straight home, cleaning it, and broiling it the same evening. Before, flounder had been a dish I ordered at Baricev's or Fisherman's Wharf. That was in the days before the casinos. Before I learned to fish for flounder for myself. Sometimes they'd bite. Sometimes they wouldn't - despite my best prognostications.

Joe took me so far up river I thought he was trying to get rid of me. We left early with our fly rods. I told Joe I needed to be home by two. We got home about five. You don't quit and leave when the fish are biting. We had the ice chest full of close to 50 bream. I don't know who, but somebody down the street from the church ate well that night. Who knows how many we threw back. Joe caught the most. He was in the front of the boat with the trolling motor and got to hit the good spots first. I think he deliberately kept me in the limbs and bushes. I lost all my flies and half of his.

I went off shore twice with David Spencer. The first time, rather than end up like *Gilligan's Island,* we trolled the smoother waters on the north side of Petit Bois. It was my first time out. Until then I had only heard about "the islands". On that trip we only caught one blue-fish. But, on the next trip….!!!! On the next trip David took David Morris and me 40 miles out into the Gulf. We fished the floating grass mats and tied up to an oil rig. We caught so many fish I couldn't move the next day. We caught sharks, bonita, lemonfish, and King Mackerel. One King weighed in at 28 pounds, another at 23. But you should have seen the one that got away. It was as long as David's boat and must've weighed 1000 pounds. Okay, maybe I'm exaggerating a little, but this is a fish story. We got the fish to the side of the boat but just beyond David's reach with the hook. David swung, the hook missed, the fish took off, and then was gone. Just like that. We were left with nothing but a limp line and a story about the one that got away.

Sometimes I catch 'em. Sometimes I don't. Sometimes they bite. Sometimes they don't. But one thing is for sure, I stand a lot better chance at catching them if I go fishing than I do if I stay home. I won't catch a single fish staying at home, reclining in my comfortable re-cliner, and watching reruns of *Everybody Loves Raymond.*

Someone has observed that everything Jesus did, he did away from home, out on the road. Jesus didn't save the world by staying home. He didn't heal the sick waiting for them to come to his door. Jesus was a fisherman of people and he knew all the best fishing holes. Whether down at the temple jacking up the religious folks or out at the leper colony giving someone a clean start. Whether in the synagogue teaching the scriptures or risking his own cleanliness with the Samaritans. Each day he got in his "boat", cast his line, and saved a hurting world. Each day he left comfort behind and went where the people were, ministered to their most basic needs and showed us love. Love as it is in the Kingdom of God. Let's go fishing!

Freedom to...

There's a man who lives in the neighborhood where we live in Madison. I don't know his name or really anything about him. All I know about him is from the car he drives. On each side of his car there is a magnetic United States flag. There's another flag on the rear of the car and another on the front. There may be others. I'm not sure. From all appearances, this man from my neighborhood is patriotic. How that patriotism manifests itself in his life I can't be sure. Maybe the flags are indicative of his support of our country's military action in Iraq and Afghanistan. Maybe the flags are indicative of his support of President Bush. Maybe the flags are an indication of his support for the thousands of men and women who are serving our country and putting their lives on the line in far-away places. Maybe the flags represent the pride this man has in our country. I would guess, and this is only a guess, that this man for the most part is a law-abiding citizen and that he appreciates and enjoys the freedoms we have, for which thousands have died.

In front of my house there is an intersection of two streets. At this intersection there is a red, octagonal sign on each corner. Without giving the word printed on the sign we already know what the sign says and, more importantly, what the sign means. "STOP" a complete cessation of movement to allow the driver to look in all directions to make sure there is no other traffic approaching from any direction. It's the law. As any one of us know when we approach that red, octagonal sign, the law under which we live, and drive, says to "STOP!" No exceptions. No exclusions. At least so I thought.

Not so with the man in the patriotic car. As he heads down (and up) our street and approaches the intersection with the red, octagonal signs, he speeds right through. No stop. Not even a rolling stop. I don't think he ever touches the brake. He speeds right through.

Maybe the sign doesn't apply to him. Maybe he has a pass that allows him to violate the law and to put the lives of others at risk. Maybe he thinks the law applies only to everyone else, but not himself. Maybe

16

I've misunderstood freedom all along and freedom really is the right to do as one pleases. It just seems to me that the witness that his car is making with the flags pasted all over it – proud American, law-abiding citizen - is contradictory to the statement made by his driving – proud American, free to do as he pleases. Apparently, what's on the outside is inconsistent with what's on the inside.

Paul was pretty frustrated when he wrote his letter to the congregation over at First Church Galatia. The members of the congregation were eating, drinking, and having a merry ole time. Enjoying their new-found freedom. And in so doing had become a right exclusive bunch, oblivious to the needs of others. When a dinner party was planned, they were careful about who was on the invitation list. No sinners, no poor, no outcasts. It would be a party worthy of only the finest, the richest, the best. Oh, they loved their new-found freedom. As long as it benefited them.

Paul wrote, "For freedom, Christ has set us free... Only do not use your freedom as an opportunity for self-indulgence." (Galatians 5:1, 13b)[i] Of course, Paul wasn't talking about patriotism, or red, octagonal signs or traffic laws in general. Paul was talking about the freedom we have in Christ, the one who set us free. And Paul reminds the congregation over at First Church Galatia that freedom is a gift and with freedom comes responsibility. In the Kingdom there are no exclusions, no exceptions. Everyone is invited. Everyone is included – even those dubbed different – especially those dubbed "different." In the Kingdom everyone is responsible for the other, so that no one goes without. "...through love become slaves to one another. For the whole law is summed up in the single commandment, 'You shall love your neighbor as yourself." (Galatians 5:13c, 14)

The freedom we have in Christ is not the freedom to do as one pleases. With freedom comes responsibility. In Christ we are set free to serve. To serve one another – even those unlike ourselves. To love and serve. As the one who came to show us how to love and to serve. As this is what we profess, so let it be as we live.

Nicknames

I saw in the newspaper that "Victor" died. I don't know who "Victor" was. According to the obit "Victor" was the nickname of the man who was 70 years old when he died. "Victor" was a retired dozer driver. Also listed in the obituary column was a 54-year old retired bridge supervisor nicknamed "Boom" and a great-grandmother nicknamed "Nana." (I glance over the obituaries each day just to make sure I'm not listed.) I was captivated by the nicknames of these people. I can understand a "Nana" that's usually a good name to give to a grandmother. "Nana" is easy for a little one to say and what grandmama and granddaddy doesn't want to hear their precious ones call them by name. "Boom" and "Victor" really aroused my curiosity. How would a man earn the nickname "Boom?" Was it the tone of his voice? As a bridge supervisor did he get to play with dynamite? Did he specialize in demolition? Maybe he was a musician, maybe a drummer, on the side. After all the band at Jackson State is called the Sonic Boom of the South. "Boom?" "Victor" also gets my attention. Lots of time we hear the young folks today call someone "Loser." But, "Victor?" I like that nickname. We all want to be victors. We all want to be winners. "Victor", I like the sound of that nickname.

Nicknames are often given to a person to describe a personal trait, characteristic, or event in the person's life. Sometimes nicknames are a sign of affection, affirmation, and recognition. "Victor." Sometimes they are derogatory, cuts, ridicule, hurtful. I remember just a few things from the second grade. I remember my teacher and I still have the rock she gave me on the last day of school. It wasn't anything special really. She was throwing it away. But it meant so much to me that I still have it. I remember roller skating in the old school at Sebastopol and cutting my foot on a broken coke bottle. Mama and Daddy had to carry me to Dr. Boggan in Decatur to get stitches. The other thing a remember is my nickname given by my classmates - "Egghead." With a crew cut (remember those?) I guess my head looked a little, well I guess, egg-shaped. The nickname wasn't out of affection, I'm sure. I still think about that and it hurts a little. I sometimes feel my head's shape to see if the description was accurate. The only other nickname I came close to having was "Rusty." My Granddaddy Taylor wanted to name me Rusty. Bruce won out and Rusty didn't stick.

Nicknames are sometimes a variation on our full name - like Bill for William, etc. But many times, nicknames tell us about someone or recall a memorable event. One day I got a telephone call. The woman's voice said, "Bruce?" I said, "Yes." She replied, "This is 'Moleskin.'" Nothing else had to be said. I knew exactly who it was. Nancy. The mother of one of the youths in my youth group in Atlanta. On a backpacking trip in the Smoky Mountains, Nancy had to use so much moleskin to protect her feet from blisters, she earned the nickname "Moleskin." It stuck. And as soon as she said it, not only did I know who it was, I was taken back to that backpacking trip that changed Nancy's life. On that trip she was truly born again. She hasn't been the same since.

Nicknames tell us a lot about people and while I didn't know "Boom", "Victor", or "Nana" personally I can surmise something of their personality and individuality, the affection that family and friend felt toward them. We carry the "nickname" Christian. A label. A name. And the name Christian that we carry tells the world something about us. But all too often the name "Christian" is misused. We use it to describe something we believe, a system of faith. But "Christian" is not only a system of beliefs. "Christian" is a statement about our life, a way of life patterned after the one we follow. Being "Christian" is not just about believing in Christ. Being "Christian" is following Christ and striving to live as he lives. That's where being Christian gets tough. It's one thing to profess belief in something or someone. It's another thing to model our lives after someone, especially someone like Jesus Christ.

Maybe that's the reason we prefer the name "Christian" over the name "Disciple." We can define "Christian" in terms of belief, but we can't define "Disciple" that way. In the New Testament the word "Christian" is used only 3 times. That's right. In the section of the Bible that deals with the person of Jesus Christ and the formation of the Christian church, the word "Christian" is used only 3 times. "Disciple" on the other hand is used 269 times. The Great Commission directs the remaining eleven original disciples to go and make, not Christians, but Disciples.

Claiming to be a "Christian" doesn't mean a hill of beans if discipleship doesn't bear witness to the name we claim. Does the name "Christian" describe what we believe or a way of life we lead? There's a big difference and the world will notice.

Handprints in the Sand

It's interesting that I ended up living only a block from the Gulf of Mexico. Spittin' distance from the ocean. A stone's throw from the beach. You see, I'm a mountain man. I've never been a real fan of the beach. Heat and humidity. Sand. Salt water. In fact, when I get to heaven I want to ask God why the ocean had to be salt water. Cool, fresh water would make the beach a little more enticing. Now, there a couple of things I do like about the beach. Fresh fish, fresh oysters, fresh shrimp – fresh seafood. Fried. Grilled. On vacations with Susan and the kids, I like looking for shells, trying to find that rare specimen among all the bits and pieces scattered by the breaking waves. I like taking walks on the beach with Susan in the early morning, watching her carefully select the colorful scallop shells to bring home and arrange in displays. The air cool, the sun rising, the water clear, the bond of love warm.

On one of our early morning walks in Gulf Shores a couple of years ago, I noticed a young boy walking toward us along the beach. As the young boy walked he would suddenly fall forward and then scribble in the sand. He would get up walk along a short distance, fall forward, scribble in the sand. Over and over as he walked toward us he would repeat the sequence. Fall forward. Scribble in the sand. Get up and walk. As we got closer I saw that he was falling forward to impress his handprints in the sand. Fall forward. Imprint his hands in the sand. Scribble. Fall forward. Imprint. Scribble. Over and over down the beach.

Curious, I tried to figure out just what this kid was doing. Fall forward. Imprint. Scribble. Get up and do it all over again. I thought he was making "animal" paw prints in the sand. Arouse the curiosity of other walkers. Scare other children. "What kind of animal is walking along the beach?" Finally, we passed him just as he repeated the sequence and, as I watched, he scribbled in the sand, "I was here." Two handprints and "I was here" written underneath. All down the beach "I was here." All down the beach this young boy was making his mark. Leaving his mark for others to see. Leaving his mark in the sand.

The only problem was the boy was not completely out of the reach of the encroaching waves. Not too far behind him the crashing waves stretched out their fingers and gently washed out the handprints and words written in the sand. The moving water and the shifting sand were incompatible partners to preserve the marks in the sand. All down the beach the waves removed any evidence of the boy's passing. Not too long afterwards there was no evidence anywhere that the young boy had even been there. How sad.

His motives were credible, his intentions sincere. He, like any of us, wanted to leave his mark. He, like any of us, wanted the world to know that he had a presence in the world. That he "was here." Unfortunately, he chose the wrong medium. His method was destined for failure. His means of telling the world, of leaving his mark, was in itself temporary, momentary, fleeting. But, one thing I noticed, he never looked back. He kept moving forward, down the beach, repeating the cycle – fall forward, imprint, write. Although the waves followed him, wiping away his mark, he kept on.

One of these days, this young boy will become an adult. With a future before him, his desire to leave his mark will hopefully remain, but in a different medium, a more lasting method, a permanent means. The world will be different because "he was here." But will it be a better place or worse? Will the quality of life be enhanced or damaged? Will lives be enriched or ruined? Will people be healed or hurt?

There is no doubt that the world will be different for his having been here. Whether it will be a better place or worse is his decision. As it is ours.

The First Step

I've never been an athlete. An athletic body apparently wasn't in my genes. One can't compete on the field of athletic competition in a 5'10" body weighing in at 95 pounds. The closest I've ever come to being a competitive athlete was as a golfer. That was a long time ago. I was a serious golfer. Slammed my clubs against the ground. Sent clubs swirling through the air. Driven by a desperate obsession to get that little ball in that little hole. I played a lot of golf in those days. To play well, to compete you have to play a lot of golf. I played in a number of tournaments over the years at Decatur Country Club. Won some. Lost some.

The lack of an athletic physique didn't lessen my enthusiasm for the games. Nor did it deprive me of brief moments of glory. Occasional occasions to stand on the winners' platform as "On Decatur" played in the background and the trophies (okay, singular trophy) was handed to the coach. I played on the tennis team that won the first tennis tournament trophy for Decatur High School. Winners of the District Tournament. We were ecstatic. The outcome was never in doubt. We dominated. The story could have had a different ending, however, if another team in our class had shown up. In any event we played in the State Tournament at Battlefield Park in Jackson. Jackie and I played mixed doubles. We lost. A sneaky strategy by the other team caught us off guard and we lost our balance. I'd never seen a girl with green hair before.

Athletic competition was a regular part of our days together as friends. David had two pairs of boxing gloves, so we boxed in his carport. A couple of bloody noses later we decided to change to a different sport. We played pick-up basketball in an accessible gym and pick-up football on the East Central Community College field. Each event began with the ritual choosing of teams. Two "captains" choosing from a lineup of wannabes. I wasn't ever chosen first and my anxiety level rose as each name, other than mine, was called. I wasn't ever chosen last. There's a lot to be said about next-to-last.

On the football field my speed, agility, and moves were akin to that of a jackrabbit. At least in my mind. On the basketball court I was the assist-man for the big guns. I fought tooth and nail for every rebound. Once my head, on the way up for a rebound, met Bill's elbow on the way down with the rebound. The doctor's house was just a short walk from the gym. No stitches this time.

At the country club pool there were two diving boards, a low "spring" board and a high board. I watched in amazement as friends took the leap from the high board, did a one and a half, and entered the water precisely at the right time with hardly a splash. My single flip off the low board, never the high board, usually ended a little short or a little over. At any rate I did become pretty good at hiding the pain suffered. I preferred perfecting my half flips off the end of either diving board. I didn't make much of a splash either, but who does at 5'10" and 95 pounds. At that size a cannonball to splash the girls sunbathing on the side was pretty much a wasted effort as well.

Nowadays, I'm still no athlete. My physique has changed over the years, but it is still not a body conducive to athletics. I am an athletic supporter, though, and occasionally make some pretty impressive athletic moves and actions, generally unintentional. Recently I unintentionally practiced some of those spectacular plunges reminiscent of my Decatur County Club days. As I made my way down to the bottom of a small creek in the woods I found a series of exposed roots that made a perfect stairway to the bottom. I took my first step to the top root. The root was smaller than the others and unable to support my weight. I made it to the bottom of the creek quicker than I had anticipated. If things had gone as I had planned I would have reached the bottom, feet first. Instead, I belly-flopped. Landing belly first in the shallow water and sandy bottom. Thankfully I noticed no pain. Apparently, I wasn't hurt. My pride was intact since, as far as I know, no one witnessed the plunge. As I lay there on my stomach on the bottom of the creek and as I pulled my nose out of the sand, I noticed what an impressive close-up view I had of the sandy bottom. So, lying there I decided to investigate, to see if anything interesting or unusual was noticeable from the close-up view. Having regained my composure I stood and wandered on thinking to myself what a doozy that first step turned out to be.

"Watch that first step. It's a doozy!" is a common warning we issue when certain dangers lurk. In many and various cases that first step is a doozy. I wonder if Abram and Sarai ever questioned their first steps into the unknown. Or did Moses ever regret that first step toward the burning bush. All the planning, risks, and first steps that led to that great first step when Neil Armstrong stepped on the surface of the moon. First steps. They're a doozy. On a Sunday morning the first step toward the altar to accept Christ. A phone call to a recovery center when you first admit you have a problem with alcohol or drugs, illegal or prescription. A letter of acceptance from the college you prefer. Driving away as your son or daughter waves goodbye from the entrance of their dorm miles from home. First steps. Doozies. For better; for worse. For recovery; toward addiction. For safety; toward the risk of danger. For others; for yourself. For help and healing; for same old, same old. For a new day; to cling to the past. To make a difference; to make excuses. For God; for yourself. That first step, for good or for ill, makes all the difference. Either way, "Watch that first step. It's a doozy!"

Ford 2600, Episode 1

The tractor battery was as dead as a doornail. When I turned the ignition key, it wouldn't hit a lick. I had driven the tractor down into the woods on a trail just wide enough for the tractor to work on clearing limbs along the trail. I turned the engine off while I worked on the trail. When I returned to the tractor to leave, I climbed aboard, steadied myself, hit the ignition... nothing. Nothing. And there I was down in the woods on a narrow trail with a dead battery and... the tractor facing away from the access route. Even if I could get a rescue vehicle to it, no jumper cables would be long enough to reach from behind the bush hog that was behind the tractor. I couldn't get alongside the tractor because there was a pine thicket to its right and a brush thicket on its left. I was in a pickle. I didn't want to go ask for help. It's a man thing, you know.

By grabbing the large tires on the tractor, I was able to move the machine down the trail a little bit to a point where the trees to the right side were fewer and smaller. I angled the tractor and began clearing out an area to park my rescue vehicle within reach of the jumper cables. I even cleared a path between a large pine tree and the bush hog that I thought would be wide enough. After moving the tractor and clearing the space I walked back to the farm house to get my rescue vehicle and jumper cables. My rescue vehicle was Mr. Johnson's truck.

Oh yeah, the truck. 1990 Ford Ranger. Four cylinders. Street tires. But small enough to negotiate the trail. That is, if the brakes were no longer locked. When I had left it earlier, it wouldn't go forwards or backwards, I figured out that the brakes were locked against the brake drum. Hence, the lack of mobility and the smell. If the truck moved the only obstacle I faced was whether the truck had the power to make it through the roadside ditch and up and over a small bank before crashing into the woods. The first try failed. So, I backed up across the road, hit the gas, hit the ditch, hit the bank, and hit the trail.

When I reached the tractor, I discovered that the access between the pine tree and the bush hog that I thought was wide enough for the truck wasn't. When I tried to back the truck up, so I could widen the path, the truck was stuck. Not enough power, street tires, and light in the rear end. Worst of all, I was alone. There I was down in the woods with a tractor with a dead battery and a truck stuck and wedged between a pine tree and a bush hog.

Since the pine tree was too big and too close to the truck to cut, the only solution was to move the bush hog. If I could take one side of the bush hog loose from the tractor, I could move it aside enough to get the truck by. I never thought about lowering the bush hog to the ground first, but that's the position it assumed quickly with the help of gravity. I never thought about moving my foot either. No bones were broken.

Finally, I was able to move the truck forward enough to get alongside the tractor where the jumper cables would reach. The tractor cranked. With the tractor running I could use the tractor to pull the truck out. I drove the tractor down the trail to a place where I could turn it around. I maneuvered it around the truck, attached the chain, and, running back and forth between the tractor and the truck, I was able to get it unstuck. But it still wouldn't back up the trail. Not enough power, street tires, and light in the rear end. Even after repeated tries and cutting down a few pines trees, I was unable to turn the truck around. Finally, getting it moving I hit the gas and high-tailed it up the trail… in reverse. I whipped it around once out of the woods, sailed over the bank, and plowed through the ditch and didn't stop until I was back at the farm house. I walked back to the tractor I had left running and drove it home as well.

Call it a human thing or a man thing or a Taylor thing. All are probably appropriate. I like to think of it as a human thing. We, as humans, seem to have this innate belief that there is no pickle that we can't get ourselves out of. We believe that through ingenuity, perseverance, and determination there is no situation from which we are unable to save ourselves. But, there is one. Only through the outstretched, crucified arms of Christ can the chasm between us and God be bridged. Only through Christ can we be reconciled to God. There is no human ingenuity, perseverance, or determination that can save us from the jam that we are in. Only God can. And does.

Victory at Last

I did it. I finally did it. I left the farm with the tractor tucked safely back in the shed. Hard to believe isn't it. After so many mishaps, dead batteries, clogged fuel lines. After having left the farm time after time frustrated, exhausted, and a dead tractor off down in the woods. Hard to believe I was actually able to leave the farm only exhausted after a day of bush hogging and even a little time for fishing. I really did it.

I hadn't been to the farm in quite some time and I needed a little time away. Solitude. Down time. When one's job demands the constant expense of emotional and mental energy, physical labor is a good diversion. Sweat. Cleansing pores, as well as, heart and soul. Physical exertion to clear one's mind to think clearly, discern, process. Not to mention cutting and clearing where the summer growth of weeds was in danger of taking over the farm – the old Johnson home place.

The home place is quiet now for the most part. Just the hum of wasps and bees and the occasional scampering lizard scorching its feet running across the hot, tin roof. Over the last few years the home place has been quiet and still. Years ago, it had been home to a family of fourteen – mama, daddy, and twelve romping, stomping kids. The Johnsons. I bet it wasn't still and quiet then. Long afterwards, Papaw kept cows and cats at the farm and maintained a sizeable, productive garden. In the early years of our marriage, Susan and I enjoyed the fresh veggies and home-grown beef. As Papaw aged the cows were sold and the garden got smaller and smaller, until it, too, disappeared and weeds took over. Papaw kept the place clean as long as he could. As a vocational agriculture teacher of a bunch of unruly junior and senior high students, the farm was his get-away place, too. Physical labor, sweat, and solitude. Now with his passing it has been passed to me to keep clean and care for.

After taking care of a few odds and ends for Mimi and gathering up what gear I needed from town, I headed the eight or so miles out into the country of red dirt, heat, bugs and solitude – just what the doctor ordered. I cut the weeds and grass, actually more weeds than grass, that had grown up in the old garden plots and around the old house. I pulled poison ivy from the chimney and briars from the old boxwood shrub. My weed eater spruced up the areas close to the house and a little herbicide applied should do what the weed eater didn't. It looked nice when I cranked (yes, you heard correctly, cranked) the tractor and headed for my next objective.

I don't know when the north power line right of way had been cut. I don't think I have ever cut it. The weeds were head-high, so I attacked it with a vengeance. Up and down the power line. Back and forth. The weeds falling before the powerful machine and chopped into mulch by the whirling blades. Up and down. Back and forth. There was the sense of satisfaction of a successful, well-done job. Yet, I was always wary. Always listening to the sound of the engine. Trying to decide if the changes were due to the strain of cutting deep brush or was it going to happen to me again. It had happened so many times before that I knew the sound the engine would make to signal the impending doom. It had happened so many times before that I knew about how long I had if it was going to happen again. And that time was growing nigh.

The tractor survived the power line and I steered the tractor toward the trail that marks the boundaries of the farm. As I trudged along the path I had a sense of foreboding. It was along this trail that it had happened to me last. The revving and slowing of the engine. Finally, the sputtering and death of the tractor. My attempts and repeated attempts to revive the powerful machine before driving off, leaving the tractor dead in the woods. As a neared the spot of the previous misadventure I grew more apprehensive. Would it happen as it did before?

I could have avoided the risk and left the tractor in the barn. I could have steered clear of any problems and stayed at home. I could have saved myself the worry and paid someone to do the work for me. I could have left the farm no different from the person that I was when I went. But, I'm a risk-taker. A gambler, of sorts. I tend to have an optimistic perspective, believing that this time will be different, better. (It may or may not be.) I'm not afraid of failure, of risk, of change. It's how I grow. It's how we grow.

I passed the ill-fated spot. The tractor purred like a kitten. Actually, it roared like a lion. Not this time. Not on this day. At the barn, I tucked the tractor safely and securely back in its shed. I did it. I really did it. I took the chance believing it could be done and it was. Having taken the chance, I now have the confidence I can do it again. And I'll try. Regardless of the outcome. Win, lose or draw, at least I'll try.

Not This Time

Ford 2600. Now I know. After the previously written accounts of my misfortunes and adventures with my tractor, some have asked what kind of tractor I have. Because I never knew Susan's dad to own any other brand of car, truck, or tractor, I knew it had to be a Ford. However, it is orange and Ford tractors are blue. John Deere green and yellow. Others red. But Fords are blue. My tractor is orange. I guess it probably is, as one person suggested, a retired Department of Transportation tractor. Thus, orange.

Which Ford? I really didn't know. 2000? No bigger. 3000? Now we're getting somewhere. A real man's tractor. Diesel. Complete with heavy armor to protect the radiator. Dents, scratches, and missing accessories indicative of work conducted under extreme and dangerous conditions. Bearing the wounds and scars of perilous missions. Not a tractor for the light-hearted. I figured it to be a Ford 3000. I didn't know for sure until my last visit to the farm and the latest episode of my tractor adventures.

Early on Friday morning, I found the tractor parked in the same spot I had left it for dead. The mechanics had done their work and returned it in time for my next work day on the farm. Out in the light of day, as opposed to the dusty, darkness of the tractor shed, I saw it. Emblazoned down each side of the tractor in bold, traditional script – Ford F2600. I felt kinda stupid. All these years it had been in plain sight. But, I guess that's the way it is for any of us. Preoccupied. Busy. Distracted. Habituated. Comfortable. We miss something significant, meaningful, fulfilling – even when it's right there in plain sight.

Even though I had other plans that morning, I had to go and check out the tractor first. The curiosity was just too much. Okay, it was more than curiosity. It was the excitement that maybe, just maybe, my tractor was at last repaired. I climbed on the seat, inserted the key, moved the stick shift into neutral, turned the key – nothing. No problem, I had jumper cables, a truck with a strong battery, and space to work with. I had learned long ago to leave space to work with. A lesson that had not come easily for me.

Borrowing power from my truck, the tractor roared to life. But, how long would it live? Would this day be any different than before? Or

would I end the day roasting marshmallows over the smoldering remains of a Ford 2600 tractor?

I started cautiously staying near the old farm house. As someone
said, kind of like an electric lawn mower. Not venturing too far from
level, open land. Constantly listening for any change in the sound of
the engine, a sound I have learned signals the impending demise of the
machine. After the yard and the old garden, I ventured further away
from the house to cut some "poke sallat" growing in a clearing down in
the woods. I know I could have cut the weeds with a hand tool, but this
was about more than just cutting weeds.

With each pass of the bush hog, I gained confidence that this trip
was going to be different. I steered the tractor down into the thicker
woods. Weaving my way through the pines I negotiated my path to
clear the briars and small trees. Even though I felt more comfortable,
there was still uncertainty. I had been bitten before and I always sure
that I could get my truck alongside if necessary. I continually listened
for any change in the sound of the motor. If the engine seemed to race,
so did my heartbeat. It was the telltale sign that this day would be no
different.

Unpleasant, unhappy, and difficult experiences have a way of haunt-
ing us for long periods of time, perhaps years, perhaps a lifetime.
When any sight, sound, smell or other memory associated with the
painful time is experienced, the emotions of that time surface and we
are taken back to that time in our lives. Oh, the emotions and the pain
will dim over time after successive, less painful repeats of that original
experience. But the memories stay awhile. Facing the demons over a
period of time helps. "Getting back on the horse (or tractor)" so to
speak.

My worst fears were just that fears. They were never realized. I cut
the shoulder-high weeds in the pasture down behind the barn. With
time running out and the feeling that I may be pushing my luck a bit too
far, I headed to the barn and tucked the Ford 2600 safely into its shed.

I did it. The farm looked better than it had it quite some time. Grass
was mowed, thickets were cleared, clearings were manicured. The
weekend farmer in me felt satisfied, gratified.

Just goes to show what can be accomplished when all the parts func-
tion properly. And there are a lot of parts! When all the parts are
working, which means they are also working together with the other
parts, it's amazing what can get done. Effectively. Efficiently. But let

just one part fail and the effectiveness of the whole machine is compromised. The machine is only as healthy as the individual parts. The machine is only as proficient as each individual part, functioning as it is designed to do and working in cooperation with all the others.

Sure, I'm talking about a tractor. But, I could be talking about the Church.

Spittin' Seeds

I was later leaving than I had planned. When I got to the entrance gate, my key wouldn't work – the landowner had changed the padlock. Rather than driving in, I had to walk. Even though beavers and the summer dry spell had drastically reduced the water level in the first pond I was able to catch a couple of small bass. But it didn't take long to fish the small pond. That's alright, the other pond was just a short walk away. I had come prepared. I had a boat plug in my tackle box and I had carried along a small paddle.

When I got to the second pond I discovered mats of grass and algae floating on top of the water and more of the tangled moss growing beneath the surface. Undaunted, I launched the flat bottom boat, just knowing that water moccasins the size of my leg were probably lurking in the waist-deep grass. Safely in the boat I began my search for the elusive largemouth bass. The experience was an exercise in futility. On every cast, the lure landed in or swam through the grass and algae mats. After every cast, the grass and algae had to be carefully removed from the hooks and spinners. Diving lures were useless. Top-water lures were not much better. The afternoon was just not turning out as I had planned. I did manage to catch two or three more bass. But the rewards were not worth the effort. Finally, frustration won. I paddled to shore, pulled the boat up into the grass, and walked out. Not even stopping by the first pond to give it one more try. Now I had other plans.

I had noticed on my walk in that the muscadines were ripe and ready for picking. Not many, but enough to satisfy my insatiable craving for the sweet juice. I formed a basket out of my shirttail and fought the briars and brambles until my shirt was filled with the luscious fruits. Back at my truck, I threw my fishing gear in the back and poured my treasure out of my t-shirt. A Smoothie cup was just large enough to hold my cache. I rolled down the window, cranked up the air conditioner, and put some Three Dog Night in the tape deck. "Sell my shoes, mama. I've died and gone to heaven." I popped muscadines into my mouth all the way home, slowly relishing the juice of each one, spitting the seeds out the open truck window.

Just goes to show you may not get what you went for, but if you're willing to look closely enough and try hard enough, there's always something you can take home.

Gizmo

We still don't know what kind of dog Gizmo is. If truth be told, without a DNA test, it's impossible to know for sure and even the test would probably tell us what we already know. From time to time there are people who try to establish his pedigree. One has identified him as part pit bull. While he may be part pit bull and while his baby teeth are certainly sharp enough, as the scratches on my arms and hands can attest, I certainly don't think that he has much pit bull in him. He does appear to have a significant amount of boxer genes, but he does lack the muscular build and coordination of a boxer. When Gizmo runs his hind legs run faster than his front legs and he looks as if he's getting the cart before the horse, so to speak.

Some people looked at Gizmo when he was younger and surmised that he had beagle in him, and he may, but it sure isn't the predominant breed. I've never see a beagle with legs as long as Gizmo's. Just as his body growth catches up with his feet and legs and I think he has assumed his permanent stature, his legs extend again, and his feet grow almost overnight leaving his body to play catch up again.

Most likely Gizmo falls into that breed and pedigree that the American Kennel Association has yet to accept – the Heinz 57. Although for Gizmo, 57 may be too small a number. I think the new addition to our menagerie can best be described by Elvis' song, "Ain't nothing but a hound dog." But, in the end, no matter "what" he is, he's ours and has been since we found him on the side of Glendale Road.

The only birthday we have for Gizmo is the day, May 3, we saw him stumbling along the narrow city street. On Saturday morning, Susan and I were surveying the damage from the tornadoes in Union County and New Albany the evening before. At about the same time, we both saw this sad, hapless puppy making its way along the edge of the road. Without thought and discussion, I stopped the truck and Susan opened the door and lifted the lost puppy into our truck and into our lives. It seemed as natural for Gizmo as it did for us as he curled up at Susan's feet and rested from the chaos of his brief life and from what must have been a terrifying night of destruction.

Our original intentions were good and what we thought were in the Gizmo's best interest. We'd take him to the vet, have him checked over really good, and place him in the animal shelter where he would await adoption by some loving family. We were very concerned that there were no "no-kill" shelters in our area. If Gizmo were not adopted after a certain period, he would be put to sleep. Susan and I dreaded even the thought that Gizmo's life would come to that end. But one delay led to another and before we could get Gizmo to the vet and to the shelter, he nuzzled himself into our hearts.

As we examined Gizmo's physical state our concerns about the horrors and dangers of his young life were confirmed. Initial examinations indicated fire ant bites by the dozens, a rampant flea infestation, malnourishment, dehydration, an assortment of parasites, and a blind left eye. We removed almost 20 ticks that were gorging themselves on Gizmo's blood. And now after multiple appointments to the vet and a couple of months of good food, plenty of water, and love, Gizmo is a different person, oops, dog. His coat is shiny, the sores have healed, and the parasites have been eliminated. His blind eye does continue to hamper his navigation and depth perception – catching a treat in midair like the other dogs is by luck and happenstance, not skill.

Gizmo's entry into our family has not been all smooth-sailing. Chelsea, our dominant Welsh Corgi, has had the most trouble adapting to Gizmo's presence. His excitement and energy constantly infringe on her turf. And visits to the vet have had to treat the wounds of her aggressive jealousy. Max, our male Corgi, on the other hand has found a friend, a playmate, not to mention, another target to share the threat of Chelsea's wrath. Yet, over time Chelsea, too, has warmed to Gizmo's presence. They may not be the best of friends, but it is as if each has found a place in the home; both recognize the other's need and right to be here.

As Gizmo cuddles and snores on the couch beside me, I look at him and wonder. I wonder where he would be if we had not picked him up

32

on May 3, the day we consider his birthday. I figure he would have died if we had not saved him. Where would he be if he had ended up in the shelter? Who would want a dog covered in fleas, ant bites, ticks, full of worms, and blind in one eye? No identity based on papers, credentials, status, or recognition. One whose only attribute we've discovered so far is love. And that love brings joy.

As Gizmo snoozes in the silence of the house along with Chelsea and Max, I look at him and see a metaphor, a parable. Where would any of us be if it were not for the God who loves us though we have no papers, no credentials, no status? Where would any of us be if it were not for the God who loves us worms, fleas, ticks, and all? Where would any of us be were it not for grace?

Ranger Bass Boat (In memory of Lane)

I'd gotten a new bass boat. Well, it wasn't a new bass boat. It was just new to me. Lane, a friend and church member, gave it to me. Free. 1975 Ranger. Tournament hull. 85 horsepower Johnson outboard motor. Complete with trolling motor, depth finder, and a water-logged paddle. Back in the time when this baby was new, we did a lot of boating up on the Pearl River and on the Reservoir. Friends with whom we skied had bass boats with the same motor. Ranger was the forerunner of the others. Johnson outboards were the classics. 85 hp would get the skier up out of the water with a shot and get the fisherman to the honey holes in a flash. Getting the bass boat was like going back in time. A time when we would spend all day Saturday and half a day on Sunday skiing up and down the river. A time when we would fish all day on the Reservoir and not get a bite. But, nothing beat potted meat, Vienna's, crackers, and a cold coke devoured on the water.

Before taking the boat for its first run, I took it to have it checked out. Just to make sure it would crank, run, and get me back to the pier. "Ah, the first tournament hull," said the mechanic. "People used to kill for one of these boats." I was proud to be the owner of a classic. The mechanic performed routine maintenance and replaced the cranking battery. I took the boat home and carefully placed it in my garage. I bought new life preservers from Wal-Mart, bright orange kind, highly visible. I took the water-logged paddle out to dry. In the hope of

33

skiing as we did long ago, I bought a new ski rope. I waited. Waited for the first opportunity for the maiden voyage in my new boat.

My chance came on a Thursday. Overcast and threatening, yet still dry. No evening activities and Susan had a meeting that would run late. Forget the lawn. Forget the garden. Forget everything. Go to the rez. Having not boated in quite a while I wanted to make sure everything was as safe and sure as possible. At the first boat ramp I decided the water was too choppy to take a chance. I crossed the spillway to the east side. The Pelahatchie Park ramp was crowded with hotshots on their personal watercraft and speed boats. I didn't want to embarrass myself in front of those guys. I didn't know how self-fulfilling that prophecy would be. I crossed the old railroad trestle and followed the road around to the Pelahatchie Bay Trading Post. There the water was calm and only a few folks fishing from the pier. No crowds on the boat ramp. Just the place for my first excursion.

I remembered all the drain plugs. I hooked up the gas line. I had remembered the key. I removed the tie downs and backed the trailer into the water. I had decided to make sure the boat would crank before I released the last restraint. It cranked. Smoked and sputtered some, but it cranked. I left it running as I unhooked the line and set it free. Once my truck was parked and I was sure that all precautions had been taken, I climbed in and prepared to set sail. Just in case, I removed one of the life preservers from storage and placed it in the bottom of the boat. Should something happen, like the boat sink, I figured the bright orange floatation device would be floating nearby, within reach, or at least an easy swim. Or spotted by a first responder.

I puttered away from the pier and to the channel. Once in the channel I pushed the throttle forward and accelerated. I was pleased with the power, the acceleration. The boat leveled and cruised smoothly across the water. I sped out to the open waters of Pelahatchie Bay, but not far enough to be visible to the hot shots and speed boats. Back and forth, up and down the channel I went. The wind in my hair, the chilly mist of water spraying as the boat struck the waves, the smell of the outboard exhaust, the smell of the river. Just like old times. I could almost see Susan on our slalom ski (El Brute) behind the boat, smiling, cutting across the wake.

After several trips, I decided I better head for home. It was getting late and threatening rain. Once in sight of the pier, I slowed to leave no wake. I puttered along. Then a mere 200 yards from the take out, the motor quit. It just stopped. Thinking I had run out of gas, I changed tanks. The motor wouldn't crank. For a while my forward momentum carried me toward the pier where a man and a woman were fishing. Then the wind won, and forward momentum lost. The man and woman seemed oblivious to my fate. Or were enjoying it too much to help. They fished. I drifted helplessly with the wind, away from the pier. The motor refused to crank. I drifted.

Unlike a tractor, I couldn't leave the boat and walk out. Somehow, I had to get the boat to the pier. I had to paddle. Paddle? My paddle was back at home, leaning against the house, drying out. I was, literally, up the creek without a paddle. Or at least downwind without a paddle. 200 yards of wind-blown water between me and the pier. I had one option. The ski rope. So, I started paddling with the coiled-up ski rope. Inching my way into the wind. The old marine carpet rubbed my knees raw. Thorns pricked my hands as a grabbed for branches. My arms ached.

Stroke after stroke I labored to get my boat to the shore. The man and woman fished on. Another fisherman walked into the store. For help? Nope. He returned and just kept on fishing. Two men put their boat in and gave me a glimmer of hope. Only they didn't see me and went in a different direction. I hoped for an observant, compassionate passerby on the highway. But what were the chances? I was finally helped by the two men in the boat. They had not gone far, only drifted out of my sight. Their motor wouldn't work either, but their trolling motor did. I was thankful for them, that they were willing to stop what they were doing and help out a struggling brother.

It sure was a lonely feeling. Stranded. Fighting against the wind. Two feet forward, one back. People within reach, but no offers for help. I know I wasn't as prepared as I should have been. But, still. Wouldn't somebody help? I paddled. I struggled. If I was going to make it, I'd have to do it on my own. People so close yet so far away. Fighting my battle alone. Is that what we've come to? Ignoring the struggles of others? Using someone else's dilemma to somehow feel better about ourselves? Refusing to get involved? Some of us, yes, but not all.

Amazing Grace

Amazing grace how sweet the sound that saved a wretch like me. I once was lost, but now am found, was blind but now I see. Not many people will read those lines without the tune to the hymn *Amazing Grace* flooding our thoughts. In fact, most of us will read the remainder of this article with the tune and words running through our minds. That's the idea, of course. Grace. We sing about it. We hear about it. We really like the thought of it. Grace. More than just a prayer prayed before our meals to recognize that the food we prepare and the food we eat, just like everything else we enjoy, is a gift of God. That's what grace means. Gift. Something freely given. Without charge. Without deserving. Gift. Grace.

John Wesley, the founder of the Methodist Church, was big on grace. Except Wesley wasn't satisfied with just a blanket definition of grace. Wesley believed, knew, that grace was a part of every decision we make and every step we take. Everything we do we do because God's grace makes it possible. God's grace precedes everything we do. So for John Wesley, the manifestations of grace were more specifically named and defined. Thus, there is prevenient grace, justifying grace and sanctifying grace.

Prevenient grace is that grace that goes before us everywhere we go. No matter where we go, God's grace is already there and at work. No matter to whom we witness, God's grace is already there at work in that person. Preceding anything that we intend and anything we may do.

Justifying grace. That manifestation of God's grace that convicts us of our sin and enables us to see ourselves as children of God. Saving grace. Justifying grace. "By grace you have been saved through faith." (Ephesians 2:8) Born anew. Born from above.

For John Wesley, justification was just the starting point. Justification was new birth, rebirth. Through justification we recognize our alienation from God and our need for reconciliation and redemption. Just as a baby grows after birth, so do we after being justified begin a process of growth. Justification is discovering the image of God within ourselves. Sanctification is the process of growing toward perfection (in Wesley's terms), that is, seeking to fulfill the image of God within us. To become more and more like Christ.

So often we think that once we have had the justifying experience, once we have been "saved" we can sit back and rest on our laurels. Got it made now. But, in fact, once we have had the conversion experience, the work really begins. We can no longer be satisfied with the status quo, with the way things were, with the way things are. Our "goal" is now to become more and more like Christ. To live like Christ, to love like Christ, to be like Christ. As someone said, "To be little Christs." New beliefs. New attitudes. New perspectives. New relationships with others. "See, I am making all things new." (Revelation 21:5) To now know and yet to continue as before threatens to make our conversion experience a charade. "If anyone is in Christ, there is a new creation; everything old has passed away; see, everything has become new!" (2 Corinthians 5:17)

Easy? Nope! No one said it would be. Not Wesley. Not Jesus. How can we do it? Only by practicing the spiritual disciplines, prayer, reading the Bible, practicing the sacraments, worship, etc. Only within the community of faith. The Christian faith is not meant to be lived alone and in isolation. The Christian faith is not just an individual's experience. The Christian faith is meant to be lived out in community – the church. The body of Christ. Lastly, in the end, the only hope we have of making it is through, you got it, GRACE.

We like grace. As I said earlier, especially as it affects us personally. Yet, gifts are meant to be shared. Even as we receive grace and experience grace, we are called to share grace with others – not just the people we like, either. No wonder we like to hang out back at justification and seek to relive that experience over and over. That felt good. That was just about us. Not about relating to people and life in a different way. Nobody said it was going to be easy. Yet if we are going to be like Christ....

Places
I
Remember

"There are places I remember all my life though some have changed. Some forever not for better; some are gone and some remain. For these places have their meaning with lovers and friends I still can recall. Some are dead and some are living in my life I love them all."
(From "In My Life" by John Lennon & Paul McCartney)

Places I Remember

I was traveling to Hot Springs, North Carolina. The trip was to be a time of solitude, prayer, and reflection. The road to Hot Springs was my customary one, traveled many times on family, church, and various group trips, but rarely alone. The route traveled carried me along I-20 to Birmingham then followed I-59 to Chattanooga. At Cleveland, Tennessee I left the interstate for the more scenic "back roads" along the Ocoee River, mountain valleys of Murphy and Andrews, Granny Squirrel Gap, Topton, and then the gradual decline into the Nantahala Gorge. The route would lead on to Waynesville, home of Lake Junaluska, and then follow an unfamiliar, winding road into Hot Springs, NC.

As I traveled along alone, I was struck by the memories that surfaced from the deep recesses of my mind. The times I had spent over the last 50-plus years traveling along those roads and through the valleys and over the mountain tops. Some memories are restored through old photos of the rare vacations with my parents in the Smoky Mountains. Two skinny boys and a blonde-haired little girl standing by entrance signs to parks and attractions and in the middle of rock-strewn mountain streams. "See Rock City" "See Seven States" "Ruby Falls" The billboards and barn roofs enticed. We went. We saw. Got the sign for our bumper. Rare occasions when it was just the five of us. I wish I remembered more about those times. My parents returned with Kris, my nephew. We even returned with our own kids. Just to keep the tradition going, you understand. "Fat-man Squeeze" I would only understand that when we returned, and that skinny kid had evolved into an overweight father.

All along that familiar route memories surfaced mile after mile. Celebrating Ben's first birthday at Davidson River Campground. Mandy wanting to get to the "lotel." Ben's first rafting run on the Ocoee River after he reached the minimum age of 12. Susan and I paddling the Nantahala River for the first time with the Sierra Club.

41

prepared. Unequipped. Tumping into the icy waters without proper clothing. Learning the importance of trusting one's own abilities and expertise and not depending too much on another. Camping at Lost Mine Campground with my mom and dad who decided to take up camping in their retirement years. They bought a tent, cots, and camping gear. Daddy visited and interviewed the Taylors of Silvermine Road to determine if we were in any way kin. Hiking in the mountains and along the streams carrying Mandy or Ben on my back. Susan and Mandy wondering where in the world that waterfall was. There wasn't one. Camping one year at "The Ghetto," what we called another campground on the Nantahala and discovering that Mandy had cooties. We all shampooed thoroughly with a treatment soap and ended the infestation before it became an epidemic. Susan and Mandy paddling tandem while I paddled solo and Ben kayaked. The family that paddles together...

More than 50 years of memories. With my mom and dad, brother and sister. With Susan, Mandy, and Ben. With John, Jim, Larry, Ned, Charles, John... I could go on... and on, but you get the gist. Memories. Times and events that, at the moment, seemed special but not significant in the overall scheme of things. I guess memories are made at a specific time in one's life then remembered and appreciated long afterward, probably at the time when more of one's life is behind than before.

And, no, all memories are not good ones. Some are tragic. Some are painful. Some are unfortunate. Some are beyond our control. Do we play the victim or victor? Do we wallow in self-pity or rise above it? We can cling to the past and make excuses or rise above the past and make a difference. Our choice.

Whatever our past may have been, we can make tomorrow better. Many, if not most, of tomorrow's memories are within our control today. We hold within our hands today the future of tomorrow's generation. What we do today, how we spend these times with the ones we love will be tomorrow's memories. We can do a lot to influence these times which we will look back on in the future. Next week. Next year. Fifty years from now. Memories. Good or bad? Our choice. Puts a lot of pressure on the moment, I know, but what a blessing, what an opportunity to seize the present in such a way that memories are created for the future. Memories that will sustain us, strengthen us, and build faith for tomorrow, for the future that is yet vague and uncertain

Anne's Waterfall

A surprise thundershower had moved through during the night at Lost Mine Campground. In the morning the clouds had begun to break and the sun peak through. There's nothing more refreshing than a morning following a cleansing rain. With coffee and digital camera in hand I headed out. At a campsite up the road a waterfall cascades down the side of the mountain into the rushing stream below. The lush green mountain laurel was in full bloom at the base of the cascade. In the cool dampness of the early mountain morning, I pulled off my shoes, rolled my jeans above my knees, and plunged my feet into the cold water to make my way to the other side of the stream. Careful not to slip, careful not to drop my camera, I positioned myself for the right angle, lighting, and shutter speed to capture the scene. Photo Op. A Kodak moment. Tumbling water over the rich brown rocks. Lush green plants with dazzling clusters of white and pink flowers. Drops of water from the overnight rain still clinging like gleaming crystals on the leaves. Photo after photo, I snapped. The rays of the early morning sun streaming through the trees. Sunbeams reflecting off the water like glittering diamonds. Stones polished round and smooth, wet and glistening.

There was so much to experience, to see, to preserve. But the experience was more than visual. Oh, so much more than visual. The quietness of the early morning was a total sensory experience. The cold water running between my toes and splashing around my ankles. The feel of the cold, hard stone and the soft, moist earth. My body chilled in the cool of the mountain air, warmed by the fresh cup of coffee. The sound of the water falling from high above. The reverberation of water crashing over rocks and plunging into pools below. Gentle morning breezes moving through the leaves and branches. Water droplets rolling from their leafy resting places and falling to the ground below, completing their journey began in the storm the night before.

Ahhh, the smells. My favorite sensory experience. The rain had only enhanced the fragrances of the mountains. Honeysuckle. The mellow blend of honeysuckle with privet hedge. As the breezes moved down the mountain side they brought with them an assortment of smells. Galax from somewhere up on the higher elevations. The "earthy" aroma of the rich, brown, moist earth. Fir and pine. Smoke from a distant fire. Bacon frying. Coffee perking. Unidentified, yet familiar, odors that spoke to me of times past.

Memories, yes. But, also, Presence. God's presence in the present. And, too, visions, promises, and hope for tomorrow. For such is the power of the senses. To stir within us a memory of the past, a recollection of days gone by. To assure us of the abiding presence of the God of love and grace. To restore within us a vision of the future, an image of how life was and can be again. To enable us to hear the voices of God. Voices that speak in the midst of life. Messages delivered in times of need. The Spirit of God moving through the places and spaces of our lives. God speaks. We are only to hear and listen. Pause long enough and be still long enough to be receptive to the voices of God. "Be still, and know that I am God," says God. (Psalm 46:10) For God is difficult, if not impossible, to hear and know in the busyness of our lives. Be still (and quiet) and know that God is God.

In the mountains. By streams and rivers. On the beach. In a park. Sitting on the patio or deck. A cozy fire and comfy couch, with the TV off. A quiet walk around the block. Each of us has our place, our time. What is mine is not the same for everyone and I can't expect it to be. It's not the location anyway. It's our receptivity. Opening ourselves and all our senses to hear, to hear the voices of God. For God comes to us in many ways and speaks to us with many voices, if we will only pause long enough to hear. "Be still and know...."

The Falls

John and I had paddled together many times. Nantahala Falls always the climax of the day trip on the river. Our approach was to run Entrance Rapids, catch Truck Stop Eddy, catch our breath, bail the water out of the boat, muster our courage, set our line for the main drop of the falls. One particular day we were successful on our route through Entrance Rapid, but hit the eddy line of Truck Stop low, real low, too low. We made one last ditch, fervent effort to catch the eddy. Actually, the effort was driven more by panic than passion. We discovered why the bow and stern ends of a whitewater canoe have additional protection. Our over-zealous effort resulted in the canoe ramming the rocks on the side of the river. John and I, our canoe not equipped with seat belts, were thrust forward by the impact. By the time we had recovered, our boat had come under the influence of the powerful movement of the downstream current and our canoe was headed over the falls... backwards. Our strongest strokes couldn't save us. My only response in fear and dread was, "We're dead!!!"

There's a reason people come from hills and hollows and sit on the rocks alongside Nantahala Falls on summer weekends. Entertainment. Where else in the remote mountains can one spend the afternoon watching people crash and burn. Amusement. Cheap. Their presence on summer Saturdays and Sundays only adds to the paddler's anxiety. It's one thing to face the currents, hydraulics, and drop of Nantahala Falls. It's another thing to face Nantahala Falls along with the intimidation of the crowds gathered for free crash and burn scenes – live, uncut, unrehearsed. The anxiety levels of canoeists, kayakers, and rafters alike rise in anticipation of the type of amusement they will provide. Turning over in the froth of the falls is one thing. To do so in the presence of a cheering crowd is another.

On one trip I remember Charles getting a little brave in his kayak. And I commented so to Ned as we eddied behind Billboard Rock. Trying daring moves, ferries, eddy turns above the falls. Apparently unconcerned about the hazards downstream. My comments were still fresh from my mouth when Charles hit a hidden eddy midstream, flipped his boat, and proceeded to run the falls upside down. Murmurs moved through the crowd. This is what they came to see. Charles' gallant attempts to roll failed and a wet exit meant he and his boat were moving rapidly toward the falls... separately. Charles escaped via Truck Stop eddy. He caught his boat a quarter of a mile downstream.

Earlier in the year, Charles provided more entertainment. Charles was having a good day on the river. No, a great day. Confidence high, Charles went for Micro Eddy, a small eddy against the left bank in the middle of the rapid. Once in Micro Eddy the stern of the kayak actually hangs over the main drop of Nantahala Falls. Charles lost his line and went over the drop – backwards. He disappeared from my upstream view and then suddenly his boat squirted up like that whale on the Pacific Life commercials and came to rest upside down. Charles calmly set up and rolled. The crowd cheered.

Charles' great day on the river was one of my worst. I couldn't roll my kayak to save my life. Try after try I failed. Every failure followed by a cold wet exit. Until that day I had had a strong roll. But, it was like I had never rolled a kayak before. Frustrated and tired I finally quit trying. Just gave up.

Without a strong roll, the pressure of Nantahala Falls intensifies. I have seen paddlers swim the falls and come out with hands and feet looking like they had been through meat grinders. I remember a guy and his wife swimming the falls. We helped his wife to the side of the river, while he remained sprawled out on a midstream rock and his broken leg askew. I have seen people I thought for certain were going to drown in the hydraulics while I watched. There has been at least one drowning by foot entrapment. Take those images combine them with a crowd hungry for action and an Eskimo roll lost somewhere in the whirlpools of the Nantahala River and my run down the falls on this particular day looked grim, at best.

There are eight miles of river leading up to Nantahala Falls. Nantahala Falls is the biggest, hardest, most challenging rapid on the river. While a short, easy portage is always a viable, honorable decision, the day is just not complete without an attempt at the falls. Despite my inept roll, I decided to make the run. I didn't want to disappoint the crowd. I also knew despite my horrible day on the river, a good run was still possible. John's and my backward run turned out to be the driest we ever made. I knew that I may turn over. I knew that I may have to swim. I knew that I had to try. Win, lose or draw I had to try.

Once I had made the decision there would be no looking back. Nothing that had happened up to that point would matter anymore. The only thing that mattered was what I would do from that point forward. I had to forget everything that had happened and look only ahead with confidence and trust.

Coming out of Truck Stop I paddled past the upper hole and set my line for the main drop. My line was okay, but a curling wave struck my kayak broadside. My best brace couldn't hold me upright. There was a gasp in the crowd and over I went. Upside down in Nantahala Falls. None of my past mistakes and failures mattered at this point. The only thing that mattered was right now. Something clicked. Memories and knowledge hidden all day surfaced and my body went into motion almost by instinct. I rolled. Success. No. Survival. All my prior failures and former mistakes had been washed away in the cold, swift waters of the Nantahala River. Redemption. In the church, we call it grace.

Waterrock Knob

"The view is not always better at the top." That is one of lessons the staff learned on a staff retreat to Lake Junaluska in the Smoky Mountains of North Carolina. After negotiating with the workshop leaders, enough free time was awarded for some sightseeing and shopping on Tuesday afternoon. After strategically planning our escape over lunch, the Parkway Hills staff headed straight for the church van after dismissal from the session. We traveled up the highway to Maggie Valley. A stop at a pottery shop was first on our itinerary. The highway climbed as we passed popular attractions such as Ghost Town, The Stompin' Ground, and the Cataloochee Ski area. One attraction, though, would not be passed up, "The Most Photographed View in the Smokies." A self-designation, I'm sure. Complete with souvenirs.

After some photos and prying the staff away from the trinkets, we navigated the van around sharp curves to the Blue Ridge Parkway. On the Parkway we stopped at virtually every "scenic view" for additional photos of the mountain vistas. No tourist traps here. Just raw nature… and a little concrete and asphalt. Then, just in the nick of time, we found it… a real restroom. Peeling into the parking lot and screeching to a halt, a voice from the distant rear of the van a voice came, "Let's take the hike." "What hike?" A half-mile walk would lead us up to Waterrock Knob, elevation 6400 feet.

The first 0.21 mile was an asphalt trail leading to an overlook that afforded nice views of the surrounding mountains. The incline of the trail seemed somewhere near 90 degrees. Cathy and Heather headed off first. Cathy wanted to "power walk" but fearing an embarrassing encounter with other hikers, Heather convinced Cathy otherwise. Off they went at a brisk pace. Philip and I were next, although the grade and elevation separated us quickly. Beth and Angel brought up the rear. At the first overlook I found Cathy and Heather sprawled out on the ground grasping for air. "This is it! We're not going any further!" "Come on, we're half way there, now." "No!! We are not going any further!!" Not knowing whether any would follow, I started up the trail which was now rocks, roots, mud, and logs. Incline, still somewhere near 90 degrees. All along the hike there were magnificent views of the mountains, but these were not the summit where we were sure the best views would be afforded. No time to stop and look anyway.

Still not knowing if any of my hiking companions and dedicated staff members would follow me, I trekked on toward the summit. At the top there was a family of hikers resting and enjoying the view. After a few moments, Cathy and Heather appeared. We caught our breath, enjoyed the summit, and then, deciding that Phil, Beth, and Angel had stopped at the end of the asphalt trail, we headed back down the mountain. After backtracking about 100 yards we met Phil trudging along. Angel and Beth, panting and wheezing, were not far behind.

Now we could all reach the summit together. "No," said Heather, "I'm not going back." "Come on, Heather, we have to do it together." "NO, I'm not going back up there." As we set out to reclaim the summit, this time together, our newest staff member said over and over, "I hate you, Bruce! I hate you, Bruce!" On the top, photos show Angel passed out in the laps of Beth, Heather, and Cathy. Beth and Angel (having come to) struck super model poses with the mountain scenery as a backdrop, 8x10 color glossies are available for a modest price. After a short rest, we had to head back down the trail. Heather was hungry and when Heather gets hungry...

A hiker's guide says that the views from the summit are panoramic. They're not. Trees and shrubs block the views. The best views were actually along the trail on the way up. But we had missed them in our determination to reach the top. On the way down, we stopped and posed for photos with Maggie Valley now far off in the distance. Hence, we learned that the view is not always better at the top.

Reaching the summit was only a goal, but much more was achieved that cool, overcast afternoon on Waterrock Knob. Many times, getting to the top at the expense of the journey and the views along the way are not worth the price. But this time it was important for us to reach the summit. What we accomplished we accomplished together, but each at his/her own pace. And, in the end, when we reached the parking lot and, at long last, the restrooms, we had had an experience that would provide memories, laughter, aches and pains, and common ground on which we could continue to build friendships and working relationships to enhance the ministry of Jesus Christ.

Lovers Leap

High above the French Broad River overlooking Hot Springs, North Carolina is an outcropping of rock on the Appalachian Trail. The rock outcropping is called Lovers' Leap. Seems as if everybody has a "Lovers' Leap" near their town. I'm not sure if the Lovers' Leap in Hot Springs has the same legend or not. You know, a young man and woman from different backgrounds fall in love but are prevented from being married because of social customs and mores. Since they can't be together in this life, they decide to go on to the next where they can be together. So, they climb to the top of the cliff, have a last kiss, clasp hands, and jump. "Lovers' Leap."

The first day I hiked up to Lovers' Leap the weather was cold and rainy. I was alone, by the way, with no plans to jump, by myself or otherwise. I was going for the view. Due to the rain and fog I took a couple of photos and they trudged on down the Appalachian Trail toward the Pump Gap trail and then back to my room, dry and warm. On Friday the promise of clearing skies impelled me to hike to the cliff again. With no plans to go any further, I carried my camera, water, snacks, book, and journal.

The promise was fulfilled. The rain ceased. The sky cleared. The sun broke out. On the rocks of Lovers' Leap, the sun was warm, and the breezes were light. The view? Spectacular. Below me were the rapids of the French Broad. Across the river was the town of Hot Springs. A train wound its way along the railroad tracks beside the river. A flock of turkeys emerged warily from the woods and fed in a pasture outside the reach of the town. A UPS driver made his deliveries. Traffic moved up and down the streets. NCDOT workers made repairs on the river bridge. A hawk glided effortlessly catching the updrafts above the river and over the mountains. Oh yeah, mountains as far as I could see.

Across the way I could see the retreat center where I had been reading, praying, and maintaining silence all week. That regimen of the practice of the spiritual disciplines had heightened my awareness of God's presence and enhanced my perception of Christ and his ministry. Sitting there on the outcropping of rock in the warm sun and cool breezes and scanning the Gospels in my mind, I could imagine why Jesus spent so much time on the mountains himself.

I could understand with depth and insight the nature of the tempta-
tions of Jesus when he was taken up on the mountain top and shown the
surrounding landscape. "All this can be yours if you will..." Tempting? You bet. Mountains. Rivers. Rapids. Trees. "All this can be
mine?" "If you will..." It had to be hard to turn down.

I could understand with an awakened consciousness how hard it
must have been for Jesus to resist using the power at his disposal to
feed and free the hungry and oppressed. Looking down from the
heights. Seeing the houses in each village and town. Knowing that in
each house were people who were hurting. Children who were hungry.
Couples struggling to make ends meet. Parents caring for children.
Children caring for parents. Knowing that he possessed the power to
set them free, but just couldn't bring himself to use his power in that
fashion.

Sitting there on Lovers' Leap I could understand why Jesus went to
the mountaintop to teach his disciples and his followers. I could understand why Jesus took Peter, James, and John to the mountaintop to let
them witness his transfiguration, to reveal to them his divine nature, to
pull back just for an instant the curtain of eternity to allow them to see
him for who he really was. Sitting there in the silence and solitude,
above the uncertainty of life in the valley, I could understand why Peter
didn't want to leave. I didn't want to leave either. Peace. Quiet. Se-
clusion. Up there, there were no distractions, no pressure to perform,
no bills to pay. Up there, there were no financial problems, no family
trouble, no war, no hate. Up there, there was peace, quiet, solitude. Up
there, there was only me with my thoughts and God. I could understand why Jesus went there, why Peter wanted to stay.

For Jesus the mountaintops were his diversion, his escape, time for
solitude and prayer. But Jesus had to leave the mountain. Peter, James,
and John had to leave. The people in those homes, in those towns and
villages, were the people who needed to be made whole, given a second
chance, raised to new life. Jesus was needed down in the valleys, in the
low places. Wherever there was suffering, sickness, pain, death, and
sin. His healing and life-giving power would be of no use isolated and
removed up on the mountaintop.

Again, I could understand with a new perspective. I had to leave,
too. The next day was Saturday, the day I was to head for home. As
much as I wanted to stay on that outcropping of rock on the warm,
sunny day high above the troubles of life, as much as I wanted to stay

in the peace and quiet of Hot Springs, I had to leave. My ministry was back home. Where people hurt, where people are lonely, where we can respond to the needs of the world together in the name of Christ. Ministry is here, where we will get our hands dirty, our backs will hurt, our hearts will break, our legs will tire. It is here, down in the valleys of life that people need God, that God needs me. And, God needs you.

Road to Runion

At the end of the trail were the ruins of Runion, NC, an old railroad town on the banks of the French Broad River. The trail ran for three miles along the banks of Big Laurel Creek to where it emptied into the French Broad River at the ruins of Runion. The weather forecast was for snow developing after noon. I made the short ride from Hot Springs, NC to the trailhead. With my day pack stuffed with water, "snail tracks", books, and new digital camera I set out all alone for the six-mile round-trip hike to Runion. The trail was level and easy. I made good time. I wasn't worried about snow. A hike in the snow along a mountain stream would be a beautiful and inspirational hike. After all that was what I was there for, inspiration, meditation, prayer – my personal spiritual life retreat.

One factor that I did not consider when I began the hike, however, was the absolute beauty of the stream and the complete solitude that I would experience. The rapids were fast and furious. The rocks that compressed the river into narrow channels of rollicking whitewater were large and imposing. Gravel bars offered vast selections of smaller rocks to load into my already weighty day pack for souvenirs. Every step along the trail that followed Big Laurel Creek on a cold, overcast day provided a new photo with my camera. The large rocks provided shelter and perfect spots for rest and contemplation. All this beauty and absolute solitude, too.

With only half of a short winter day to complete the trip to Runion I had a decision to make. Did I push myself for the purpose of completing the hike and making it to my goal? Did I sacrifice the beauty and the experiences along the way? Was reaching my goal worth the cost of missing what the trail had to offer one who could stop and see, and feel, and hear? The rushing rapids called me. The rocks and trees

invited me. The solitude and beauty cried to me. Stop. See. Listen.
Feel. Rest. Pray.

There were so many places to stop. So much to see and experience.
I would stop for a while and then move on; afraid I might miss something better if I didn't. Finally, I stopped for one last time. I leaned up
against the cold stone, listening to the voice of the wilderness, feeling
the wind on my face, watching the sky for snow. I read. The book was
<u>Peace</u> by Walter Brueggemann. *Shalom*, the Old Testament word that
describes the well-being of all God's creatures, peace in every corner of
creation. The hike was somewhat of a metaphor of the images of shalom. Peace and well-being.

That stop was my last, not because I was determined to reach Runion and to stop any more would deter me from my goal. The stop was
my last because I decided Runion could wait until another day. Fulfillment was not to be found in reaching some goal at the end of the trail at
the end of the day. Fulfillment and meaning were to be found in the
hike itself and the experiences along the way. Like life ought to be.

I never made it to Runion. I never took another chance that week to
complete the trail to its end. It didn't matter to me. I had had more
than I could ever have imagined. The end couldn't have made my
walk, my pilgrimage any more meaningful, any more fulfilling. I had
witnessed beauty beyond belief and found God in a new way and in a
new place. I didn't see another soul the whole day. But I had plenty of
time and space to see mine. Shalom.

Day Trip to the Pass

I don't know if I've ever seen so much stuff in one place in all my
life. On the shelves there were old books, glassware, ceramics. Glass
display cases held jewelry, trinkets, old toys. Tables were covered with
brassware, more glassware, more ceramics. Scattered around on the
floor were pieces of antique furniture, old tools, and anything else that
wouldn't fit on shelves or in glass cabinets. As awed as I was by the
quantity of stuff, I was equally impressed by the variety of stuff. Not
new stuff. Old stuff. All of which was for sale for a price.

When our close friends, Phil and Ann, arrived for a short visit to the
coast over the New Year's holiday, we spent an afternoon together

touring the coast before attending a holiday Broadway-like show in the evening. We traveled west along Highway 90 to the coastal towns of Long Beach and Pass Christian. Places that none of us had ever been, much less explored.

Having a couple of shopping experts, okay fanatics, in the car, our objective was to locate unique shops along the scenic stretches of beach. A lunch of fried seafood (is there any other kind) at a Long Beach restaurant fueled our engines and stuffed our bellies. Being a holiday period, many shops were closed. So, we ventured off the beach to the city streets in search of antiques, gifts, whatever we could find that our little hearts desired.

In downtown Pass Christian we finally made our first stop. I don't remember the name of the shop but from the outside it appeared to be just what we were looking for. A pedestal bathtub served as a flower pot under the front window. In the window hung a beautiful piece of stained glass. The mismatch of the two prominent features was a fore-boding of what awaited us inside.

When we walked through the doors, I was overwhelmed by the stuff. Shelf after shelf of ceramic ditties, trinkets, salt & pepper shakers. Candy bowls, cookie jars, mantel pieces. Toys rusted with age, dented with wear and tear – not plastic, for these toys pre-dated plastic. Aisles blocked by displayed items – old tools from the days of an agri-culturally-centered culture, from the days when every community had its own cotton gin, gristmill, country store. Tools and cookware when every family lived off the land – milk from their own cow, vegetables from the garden, meat from the barnyard.

We wandered down the aisles and through the cubicles with wide-eyed wonder. Like children in a toy store. What appeared to be a con-verted, old, small house from the outside became what seemed to be an endless array of hallways always leading us on. I halfway expected to find myself in another dimension or lost in the caverns of stuff never to return. I was transported to a distant time and place that somehow seemed familiar.

Finally, it dawned on me why I was so moved by the experience. As I wandered, it was as if I was moving from room to room in my par-ent's home. What I was seeing displayed were the same items that they displayed in their own living room, den. The tools were the tools my daddy used in the yard and in the garden. The cookware was the same my mama used to make home-made biscuits, fried chicken, cornbread.

As I moved through the cubicles and down the aisles, it was like I was moving through the grottoes of my parents' lives and into the years of my past.

All of a sudden, the "stuff" became more personal and I realized that I was not shopping but seeing the lives of people, people like my parents, on display, for sale. All the items in that shop came from an estate at some time in some place. All the items in that shop represented someone's lives, like the lives of my parents. The things they not only worked with, but the things they worked for. The things they valued and the things they cherished. Things that were functional and things that were decorative. In the end, the things they left behind.

When we left the shop, I was left with memories and thoughts. Memories of the lives of my parents who were now gone, nothing left but a few trinkets, tools, and stuff we saved. The rest sold at a garage sale to raise money for the building fund at the church they called home.

I was left with thoughts about my own life and the stuff I cherish, value. Thoughts about my priorities. The stuff I'll leave behind. I was left with thoughts about my own life. Is that what my life will be reduced to when I'm gone – stuff stuck away on shelf somewhere? Stuff for sale in a dusty little shop for anyone willing to pay the price? Or will I, can I, leave behind something of more lasting value, a legacy that will enhance the lives of future generations, and a world that is better for me having been here? Preferably, can WE?

The Road to Nowhere

I guess I've been traveling to the Great Smoky Mountains virtually all my life. I vaguely remember what old black and white photos from my parents' cedar chest show in the highest definition of Polaroid film. Three kids, a beautiful blonde daughter sandwiched between two skinny little boys with close-cropped "crew cuts" in front of the sign that announced arrival to the Great Smoky Mountain National Park. Photos of the homes of friends nestled in the cloud covered mountains. Memories of wading in cold mountain streams. Family vacations so long ago that just these few shadowy memories remain. The photos are now gone as well.

Years would pass before my next trip to the mountains, our youth trip to Lake Junaluska sometime in my late teens. When I began work at Broadmeadow UMC in Jackson, my trips became more frequent. Backpacking. Youth leadership training at Junaluska. Then came whitewater rafting. Minister's week. Family vacations year after year to the point that the kids asked if we couldn't go somewhere else for a change – like the beach.

I have made so many trips to the Great Smoky Mountains over the last 25 years, that I thought I had seen it all. Charley's Bunion. Chimney Tops. Spence Field. Thunderhead and Rocky Top. Cades Cove to Cattaloochee Cove. Smokemont to Elkmont. Backcountry campsites and the Appalachian Trail. Bear, deer, raccoons, wild hogs, skunks, and rattlesnakes.

Our trips usually include one unknown road. Or trail. Or path. Getting lost, at least once. As on one trip, heading out of the mountain town of Bryson City we took Lakeshore Drive. In the beginning it looked like any city street. Churches. The local high school. Cozy homes with fires burning in their wood stoves. An occasional business. Then we came to where the road left the city and entered the Great Smoky Mountain National Park. As in the days of yore, a sign welcomed us. An open gate beckoned us. A second sign warned us: "The Road to Nowhere."

Now, as enticing as the welcome sign was and as attracting as the open gate was, neither was as tempting and alluring as the sign, "The Road to Nowhere." Needless to say, we just had to go. Along the way the road was just like any other mountain road. Well paved with asphalt. Clearly-painted lines of demarcation between east and west bound lanes. Beautiful vistas that provided scenic views of distant mountains, rivers and lakes, and steep ridges descending to the valley below. A quiet walkway. The trailhead for the Noland Creek trail. The trail, not surprising, follows Noland Creek. The trail is flat and wide, following the clear, cold, rushing waters of Noland Creek. The trail is deceiving for it will become narrower and steeper. It must, in order to reach Clingman's Dome, the highest mountain in the Park. I'm sure that for those who make the hike the end is well worth the aches, sweat, and fatigue that accompanies such a strenuous trek. But at least it goes somewhere, if one is willing to stay the path.

Susan and I hiked a short piece up the trail enjoying the thickets of rhododendron along the stream, the smell of moist leaves in the chilly, morning dampness, the sounds of the cascades over the stones. We walked, sauntered, really. Chatted. Took pictures. Then returned to our car and "The Road to Nowhere."

If we had consulted maps and investigated this road we traveled, we would have known that it is truly the road to nowhere. Less than a mile from Noland Creek, we saw another sign that said, "Parkway Ends Ahead." And there, before us was a barricade. Just beyond the barricade a completed tunnel cut its way through the mountain, only for the road to end on the other side.

The road had tempted us in the beginning, amazed us along the way, but it went nowhere in the end. We looked back upon the eight miles of highway behind us, with nothing in front of us. How much money had been spent to carve a highway through the wilderness along the ridges of the Appalachian Mountains? To excavate tunnels through solid rock? To erect enormous, concrete bridges to span mountain streams? How much was spent in time, money, and other resources to create a road that goes nowhere!!

One can look at it as governmental waste. One can look at it as an unfulfilled promise to the mountain people. One can also look at it as a metaphor of life. Susan and I received mixed messages at the beginning of our journey. We were welcomed, yet we were also warned. We thought the welcome came from people we could trust. We took the chance – enjoying the views along the way, the adventures of new places, new sights – new paths. Spending time and resources freely as if there were no tomorrow. Only to find in the end that the road on which we were traveling was a road to nowhere.

I admit we enjoyed the adventure, the unknown. We had fun along the way. Saw new sights. Discovered new places. And there were lessons learned. Lessons that make a difference only if the lessons learned are also lessons remembered. And we were lucky. Lucky that the road to nowhere didn't have a more dangerous ending. No sign of warning. The darkness of the tunnel with no way out. An abrupt end of the road with a sheer cliff that dropped off into eternity.

Back in town there's a stop light. One road goes north and east to other towns and destinations along the way. The other road goes south and west. It's the road to nowhere. Only a prayerful, discerning person guided by the Holy Spirit, utilizing the aid of directions on an accurate map, and the support of family and friends can know the difference.

Billie Joe's River

For some reason that my subconscious has yet to release, whenever I hear *You Made Me So Very Happy* by the group Blood, Sweat, and Tears I remember driving along the street in front of Charles' house. *Susan* by the Buckinghams takes me back to the time when my wife, Susan, and I were dating. *Spooky* by Classics Four, *It's A Beautiful Morning* by The Rascals, and many other songs from the 60s and the early 70s possess the power to summon forth powerful memories of my teenage years. Music is like that. It carries us back to another time, perhaps a simpler time, a more romantic time; however embellished they may be in our recollections.

When we learned we were moving to New Albany, I researched the area on the internet and was impressed to find The Park by the River. Complete with walking trail, biking trail, Frisbee golf, playground, and... a river. But not just any river. The Tallahatchie River. The river mystified in Bobbie Gentry's song from 1967, *Ode to Billie Joe*. Reminiscences from my junior year in high school bubbled up and the same questions are again asked: Who was Billie Joe? What were he and the storyteller throwing off the bridge? Why did Billie Joe jump? Which bridge over the Tallahatchie River was the bridge in the song? In any case the Tallahatchie River has been a river of intrigue and mystery ever since the song was released and even more so now that I live on the banks of the enigma.

I know where the Tallahatchie River ends. It ends where all rivers in Mississippi end. The Gulf of Mexico. How it gets to its ultimate destination is the Tallahatchie River's own unique story. One Friday I set out on an adventure of sorts. If the river holds so much fascination for us, I had to know where it began. I set out to find the headwaters of the Tallahatchie River.

I left the city limits of New Albany and traveled east on Highway 30. Upon reaching the sprawling city of Keownville, I headed north for my first upstream crossing. Disappointedly it didn't look a lot different from what I see every day from the Bankhead Bridge. At the next county road, I headed east for my second encounter. A little smaller, but not a not different otherwise.

For a good hour I zigzagged out of Union County and into southern Tippah County. North. East. North. West. Each county road carried me across the clear, flowing waters of Billie Joe's demise. Some roads were paved, some not. One road was so eroded I wondered if I had ventured onto some dead-end road to nowhere. I still think I heard banjo music. Finally, the two-rutted road also crossed the river, now no more than a small creek or ditch. Still recognizable as the Tallahatchie by its channelized embankments. Flowing through flat cultivated farmland.

The water from that small creek in southern Tippah County flows relentlessly until it stalls for a while in Sardis Lake. You can dam it, constrain it, restrain it, restrict it but only temporarily. The river will eventually reach its final destination. After finding its way through the spillway of Sardis the waters of the Tallahatchie merge with the Yalobusha to form the Yazoo. Gaining volume, the water constantly interacts with the embankments along the way gathering soil, silt, and other debris that becomes a part of the river's unstoppable dash, okay, stroll, to the Gulf.

Somewhere far south of here, the great Mississippi River dumps its water and load of silt into the Gulf of Mexico. Mingled with the waters of the Mississippi, the Missouri, and countless rivers, creeks and streams is the water of the Tallahatchie River. In the end it is a far different river from that small creek borne in the hill country of Union and Tippah Counties. At the end the narrative of the river is not just one story, but an anthology of short stories told and gathered along the way. Each story read and understood in the rich depository of silt of the Mississippi River delta.

Ahhh! The Tallahatchie River. Billie Joe's river. A river of mystery, intrigue, and romance. Our river. Our story. A metaphor of life.

Evensong

The house is really nothing elaborate. Wood frame with lap siding. Rectangular. Two-story. A small covered entry. A covered deck on the back. The inside is open, warm, and cozy. The appearance of the house was determined more by the price than by our desires. We would have loved for it to be log construction with dormers, wraparound decks, wood-burning fireplace, the works. When the estimates came in, the design became more simplified.

What was ultimately most important to us was not the appearance of the house, but what the location of the house would provide for us. The house is located at the dead-end of a county road. In the summer no other house is in view, although there are others nearby. A small mountain stream forms the boundary between our property and the road. Our four and a half acres provide a quiet, secluded hideaway.

We knew our little cove was a special place the first time we saw it. Before the house was built we would spend time on our land sitting, dreaming, planning. Before the house was built we named our place Evensong, for it was a place from the very beginning where we felt especially close to God and each other. Evensong is the name for Evening Prayers in the Anglican tradition, used especially when the prayers are sung. The liturgy is conducted in the late afternoon or early evening. Vespers.

The twilight time of day is just a special time for me. Enchanting. Holy. Maybe it's that the whole world seems to breathe a sigh of ease and delight at the closing of the day. Work is done. Families gather. A meal is shared. Fires are lighted. Hearths and hearts are warmed. (At least in our most romantic dreams, our deepest memories, or our collective unconscious.)

At twilight, I'm taken back to a simpler time, a younger time. A time when Mason jars were filled with lightning bugs captured as they rose from the grass damp with the evening's first dew. A time when the cousins gathered at Grandmama and Granddaddy Taylor's house (only next door) and played "Ain't No Bears Out Tonight." Ringing around the house knowing at any time the older boys would spring from their hiding places to thrill and chill the younger among us. Get us running as fast as our little feet could carry us and then pull the water hose taut and send us sprawling out on the ground. Giggling.

I can't think of twilight without thinking of campfires with friends. Watching the sun set from the overlook at Silar's Bald. Giving Susan an engagement ring on a hilltop as the sun set over Decatur. I can't think of Evening Prayers, Vespers, Evensong without remembering a "skint-headed" little boy with braces sitting between his mama and daddy holding a Cokesbury hymnal during evening worship. We sang the old hymns of the Methodist tradition. The preacher preached a shortened sermon. I watched as the setting sun illuminated the stained-glass rose window in the west wall above the chancel. The brilliance of the colors changing through the spectrum like a kaleidoscope.

At Evensong, our little piece of God's creation, the lightning bugs still rise with the early evening dewfall. They twinkle in the encroaching darkness as the stars emerge from their hiding places in the sky overhead. The full moon rises over a distant mountain top. The colors change in response to the failing light and the cooling mountain air. The stream down below cascades over the stones and in the splashing and gurgling, if one listens closely enough, the melodies of hymns ascend through the trees. A chorus of crickets and tree frogs sing along. Holy space. Holy time. Amidst the soft melodies of Evensong, God speaks. Whispers of Evensong. And... because the pulse of my life slows enough to beat to the rhythm of God, I hear.

While an escape to a place like Evensong is an elixir for the ailments of a hurried life and a searching soul, we all have to find other times on a regular basis to allow the tempos of our lives to synchronize with the cadence of God. Times when we are attentive enough to hear God speak. It may be sitting in our favorite chair with the Bible in our lap, or just sitting quietly pondering, meditating, listening. It may be a play day with the children in the park. Drifting along in a boat on a lake, daring the fish to bite. Sitting in a deer stand observing life in its most elemental state. Taking a brisk walk with a friend. Strolling through the garden.

Where, when, how? It's all relative. But it is a deliberate act on our part to make it a part of our day, our life. So, we may find God's rhythm, hear God's melody and synchronize our heartbeat to the heartbeat of God.

The
Healing
Storm

The First Report

The magnitude of the storm and the enormity of damage in Decatur was enough for me. Wind toppled hundred-year-old oaks and mighty pines. Many times, the direction of their fall carried them into the roof of a home or the hood of a car. Driving through the streets after the winds had subsided revealed the path of destruction of Hurricane Katrina. I couldn't imagine what devastation had been delivered on the cities of the Gulf Coast and especially our home in Pascagoula.

During the height of the storm I talked with John riding out the storm in Bay Towers where his 90 plus year old mother resided. He described the rising waters on Market Street and in the parking lot. I called Mike. The wind whirled in the speaker of my cell phone. In the turbulent water, driven by 125 mile per hour winds, he was frantically trying to get family and pets to a place of safety from the house in which they had decided to ride out the storm. Dianne called me from First United Methodist Church, her family's refuge, to tell me "your church is flooding." Water had already climbed to the first landing on the stairs leading to the second floor. In the background I heard her husband, Harry Joe, yell, "Oh, my God! There goes a Winnebago!" With these images describing the power of Katrina, what was going on at our home?

When I received the first report of the effect the storm had on the parsonage in which we lived, Susan and I were in the parking lot of the Newton Walmart the day after landfall. I called Alice and asked if she could tell me anything about our home. Her response was beyond belief, unimaginable, inconceivable. "I'm walking through the remains of your house now. There's nothing left." "There's nothing left." Those words still reverberate in the recesses of my mind. The truth of that statement would be underscored and verified in the days and weeks to come.

Susan and I decided to wait until Wednesday, two days after landfall, to make our way back to Pascagoula and whatever awaited us there. With gas shortages nationwide and highways closed, we knew the trip home would be adventure in itself. We waited in line in Meridian to fill both vehicles and three extra five-gallon cans with gas. It would be enough unless... We stopped in Waynesboro. Ate a burger. Walked the dogs. Convinced the bank to cash a check. Bought a few groceries and a weather radio with TV channels. The radio would be our only contact with the outside world for quite a while.

Susan and I still disagree with the route we took from Citronelle, Alabama. In either case we got to I-10. Because of flotsam U.S. 90 from the interstate into Pascagoula was reduced to one lane each way. Once in the city, traffic wasn't a problem. Neither were police or military check points. The wreckage left by Katrina was. Streets were covered, and many times blocked by the remains of people's homes. Sometimes an entire house sat in the middle of the road. Just like it had been built there. Like grave sites, concrete slabs marked the previous existence of homes. Piles of brick and wood served as the tombstone. Flooded cars were everywhere. And everywhere there the fragments of people's previous lives.

Through the maze of mud, lumber, limbs, and indescribable rubble we made our way home. Only home didn't exist anymore. The exterior bricks had fallen away. Sheetrock had either dissolved or been stripped away. The carpet had been ripped out and washed away. The contents of the house, everything that defined our home, had been flushed out by the wind-driven water of Hurricane Katrina. Furniture, gone. Appliances, gone. Clothing, except what we had with us, gone. Family photos journaling the life of our family, gone. Memorabilia from the high moments of our lives, gone. Everything, gone.

In shock we stood and stared with tear-filled eyes. Everything that defined us was gone. Everything that we valued was gone. Virtually everything in which we found a sense of identity was gone. We had lost everything. Actually, almost everything. Susan and I still had each other. We had family and friends. We had lost everything, but we were alive.

In Romans 8:28, Paul writes, "We know that all things work together for good for those who love God, who are called according to his purpose." On August 31, 2005 standing in the remains our home at 2103 Washington Ave. in Pascagoula, MS, that was our only hope.

The First Sunday After

On Sunday, August 28 the attendance at the two worship services was down from the average of 325 to about 100. The drop in attendance was due to a category-five hurricane named Katrina brewing in the warm ocean waters with her sights set on the Mississippi Gulf Coast. Those who had not evacuated were at home preparing to evacuate. Boarding up windows. Raising furniture to a higher level. Moving cars and trucks to higher ground. Packing sentimental possessions for travel north, anywhere space was available away from the expected destructive winds. After our services, the church building was sandbagged and sealed.

On Monday, August 29 none of the emergency preparations were enough to resist the unexpected surge of wind-driven water that had built to tsunami proportions out in the Gulf. Ten feet of water flooded the church all the way to the second-floor sanctuary. All the church offices and their contents were lost. In the parlor the baby grand piano floated. The pre-school rooms were gone. The safe, full of church records, was a slimy mess.

Everything was gone. Not just the church. Ninety percent of the homes and businesses in Pascagoula were destroyed or damaged. Along Beach Boulevard and four blocks inland, most homes were reduced to a concrete slab, a thicket of creosote pilings, or a skeleton of wooden studs. Streets were blocked by debris ranging from splintered wood to whole houses moved from their foundations. Everything was covered with a sludge mixture of sewage, mud, and sea water. Leaves were blown from those trees that remained standing. People wandered around like zombies. Images, mental or digital, can't do justice to the scene of utter destruction. In addition, virtually every home all the way to the railroad and many beyond were flooded and soon the streets became like tunnels through piles of muddy carpet, moldy sheetrock, and soggy furniture. Tohu wa-bohu.

Those first days are still a blur. We became scavengers. Searching for anything that may have once occupied a space in our homes. Anything we found was a treasure. When you have lost everything, anything you find and can claim as your own, broken or whole, is an object of immense value.

Until the luxurious FEMA trailers began to arrive, people stayed wherever they could find a space. In tents. In campers. In rooms in their muddy, flooded homes. Some were "lucky" to have a motel room. Many, like us, stayed with family or friends. In the Walker commune, though the house had flooded, there were the homeowners, Russ and Alice, son Matt with wife April and daughter Allie, Russ' parents Katie and Grover, Susan and me, and anyone else who may happen by.

Before we could shower under a trickle of cold water in the house, we bathed in a neighbor's pool. Generators ran day and night, if we could find the gasoline. Remember, in August on the Gulf Coast it's not just the heat, it's the humidity. There were the bugs. Houseflies. Mosquitoes. Drain Flies. I'd never heard of drain flies before. Then there was the smell. Ugh, the smell!

In the midst of all the chaos and confusion, another Sunday was fast approaching. Where would we worship? How would we worship? How would we get the word out? How many people would come? And... what would I say?

We gathered in the church parking lot at 9:30 on the morning of September 4, Labor Day weekend, one week after. Groundhog Day number seven. About 125 of us gathered on a hot but beautiful Sunday morning. Statistically, ninety percent of the people there suffered the loss of their homes and/or possessions. Worshippers sat in lawn chairs, on cars, on the pavement. Many stood. The Walker Commune arrived in a trailer pulled by a four-wheeler.

We sang, from memory, the hymns of our faith. Shared updates on loved ones not in attendance. Offered advice and information on the first steps out of the mud and debris. Being good Methodists, we received an offering. Ashlynn passed the hat. How much we received, I don't remember, and it doesn't matter. People offered to God their gifts. With damaged homes, virtually no possessions, and financial uncertainties looming, people still acknowledged the Source of all we have and all we are.

I climbed into the back of a pickup truck. Standing on the tailgate, dressed in one of the few sets of clothes I had, I turned to the only scripture I felt spoke to all of us on that first Sunday after. I went to the same place to which each of us had to return – the beginning. I read the first verses of Genesis chapter one: "In the beginning when God created the heavens and the earth, the earth was a formless void (Tohu wabohu) and darkness covered the face of the deep, while a wind from God swept over the face of the waters." (Genesis 1:1,2) On that first

Sunday after, a "how" translation of the verses would not speak to the victims of Katrina but an affirmation of the creative power of God would. Just as the affirmation had offered hope to the exiles in Babylon. "How" God created the cosmos would offer no hope, but that GOD had the power to bring a new creation out of nothing but chaos and confusion, would. Our only hope was the power of God to create a new world, a new life when everything else, every other power we trusted, could not. Only God could take the splinters, mud, and debris of our lives and mold them into something new, something good. The God who had brought a new creation out of nothing, who transformed death into life, would do it again. And God did. The good news is... God still does.

Green Mug

Every morning the first thing I do is make my coffee. Every morning I get out of bed, walk to the kitchen, measure two scoops, and pour in four cups of water. That amount makes two cups in my favorite mugs. Considering my morning routine, it's understandable that a coffeemaker was one of the first purchases I made when we moved into the "Pink Palace" after the hurricane. It's also understandable that a coffee mug was purchased since all my mugs were lost. I made a trip to Wal-Mart and purchased the essentials – clothes, a coffeemaker, and a mug. Every morning in the pinkness of our camper I drank my two cups of coffee from that green ceramic mug. No logo, no cute little saying, just green ceramic. Not even very pretty.

Since then my mug collection has grown to include some of my favorite mugs we found under bricks and debris. Now in the mornings I have a choice from which mug I'll drink my coffee. But, every now and then, I have to pull that big, green ceramic mug out of the cabinet, savor a cup of coffee, and cherish the memories of the Pink Palace. It's not really the memory of the camper I cherish. It's those days and first weeks following the storm. A time when despite the destruction, the losses, and the grief, good things were happening. Lessons were learned – the value of life versus the value of stuff, the appropriate priorities for happiness and fulfillment. The centrality of our faith. We were nicer to each other. Everyone waved at everyone else. Everyone waited for each other at intersections, nobody would go first. We were the people we ought to be.

Every now and then I pull out that big, green mug, drink a cup of coffee and remember how things were in the weeks immediately following Katrina. I savor the coffee and I savor those memories. But, as I drink from that mug, I worry. I worry that the lessons will soon be forgotten. We'll take life for granted once again. We'll replace the lost stuff with new stuff. Our priorities will revert back to where they were. And, maybe worst of all, we'll forget how we ought to treat each other unable to see others as brothers and sisters traveling along the same road together. The danger of forgetting is real, unless we make a conscious effort to remember.

As human beings we typically have a short memory. God knows that, so God gave the Hebrews the gift the Passover Feast to be celebrated annually to remember how God delivered them from the cruelty of the Egyptian pharaohs. God knows we suffer from spiritual amnesia, so God gave us the bread and the cup, lest we forget how much God loves us. God knows our memories are short-lived. No wonder when Jesus broke the bread with his disciples on the night he gave himself up for us, he said, "Do this in remembrance of me." And then after supper, he passed the cup around the table and said to his closest friends, "Drink from this all of you in remembrance of me."

Let us never forget.

Piano Hammer #41

Had it not been for the events of August 29, 2005, I really would have wondered how in the world the object got where it was. But because of the devastation wrought by Hurricane Katrina in Pascagoula, and particularly along Beach Boulevard, I wasn't surprised in the least. I was riding my bicycle in a seemingly futile effort to shed a few pounds in my quest for Dee's banana pudding. You see, Jack and I had a bet on which of us could lose the most weight. The winner (or biggest loser) got Dee's banana pudding.

I had peddled with the wind down Beach Boulevard and made my turn back into the wind just past Pascagoula Street. Struggling into the wind, I watched the pavement pass under me as opposed to gazing out on the beauty of the early morning Gulf of Mexico. With my eyes cast down, I caught a glimpse of a padded felt hammer from a piano lying in the walking path of Beach Blvd. Having found Susan's Yamaha studio piano in someone's back yard a block and a half from our house, I wasn't surprised to find the hammer where I did. Nothing much surprised any of us those days. I wheeled my bicycle around and stopped over the hammer, the hammer for key #41. Counting from either end of an 82-key keyboard I ended up on C- sharp (or D-flat) in the middle of the keyboard.

I don't know why I was compelled to stop and pick up the hammer. Even though it was in pretty good shape considering what it had been through, what was it good for? Why pick it up, take it home, and glue the broken parts firmly back on? It's not like I'm going to keep it because one of these days I might have some use for it. What good is one piano hammer without the rest of the piano? There is no string to strike to produce a C-sharp, or any other note for that matter. Even if I had a string for it to strike, what good is a one-note piano? Ever heard a song written with just one note? Me either.

The only reason for picking up the hammer and repairing it as best I could, was sentimentality. The sadness of Susan's lost piano. The thought of a graduating senior, who played in church every other Sunday, getting a new Yamaha piano as a gift from her parents. Remembering our elementary-aged daughter picking her way through her first simple pieces of music and much later as a senior herself playing the piano with the All-Superior Concert Band. The luxury of lying in bed on a Saturday night and drifting off to peaceful sleep as Susan practiced her music for Sunday morning worship. Ahh, much like going to sleep with the draft of an attic fan drawing the sweet scent of the four-o'clocks across my bed.

I thought about the hammer for key #41. I was sad for it, unable to make its music anymore – no string to strike, no other hammers to work alongside, no notes to harmonize with, nothing else. It is nothing without all the other parts that make the piano a piano. No Bach, Beethoven, or Chopin. No praise to God, call to prayer, sending forth. Only the silence of a broken piece of wood and felt lying useless on the side of the road.

In the end it was sentimentality that led me to turn around and rescue hammer #41 – the sentimental thought that it reminds me of ourselves - that we are created for community. We need each other, as different as we may be, so we may vibrate together in harmony. That sun-bleached hammer beaten by the waves of Katrina reminded me that we can do and achieve more together than we can alone. Hammer #41 reminds me that the church is not just one person, one group, but it is all the parts doing their parts in concert and harmony together that make the church the church.

2103 Washington Avenue

Almost daily, even though it is well out of my way, I drive by 2103 Washington Avenue on my way to the church. Once or twice a week I'm compelled to stop even though nothing remains but the concrete slab. I pull into the driveway, park, and walk. I generally walk around the perimeter of the slab... kicking dry dirt aside... looking. Looking for what, I don't know. Something we've missed over the last eight months. Something of value we haven't yet realized we lost. Something of no value, except for the value in finding something, a small treasure. In a sense a small victory over the storm that took virtually everything we owned.

Of course, after the monstrous machines engulfed the remains of the parsonage and the huge trucks hauled off the debris we haven't found much of anything. A makeup brush. Some computer software CDs. Some corroded coins that the bank won't accept. I've started a small collection of the glass beads and crystal marbles I've found. Why? I don't really know. Memories. Something I don't understand and can't begin to explain. Just something to have, to keep, to remember.

We were able to recover the lilies Susan had planted in the front flower beds. They have traveled with us throughout our itinerancy. Huge bunches of these lilies lined the front of my grandparents' home in Decatur. After Grandmama and Granddaddy died we retrieved some of the bulbs and they've been from southwest Mississippi, to Madison, and to Pascagoula. We've lately enjoyed their blooms in the pot in which they now grow in our carport. Susan also saved other lilies, flowers, a Christmas cactus, and asparagus ferns she had planted at 2103 Washington Avenue. Plants are Susan's thing. She carries them with us like jewelry, trinkets, and treasures.

Me? I'm just compelled to stop, walk, and look. To be close. Like visiting the graves of my parents. Though they're not there, it is as close to them as I can be. Like stopping by the house where I grew up. Though we no longer own the home, it is as close as I can be to my childhood, Christmas mornings, Thanksgiving dinners, go-cart races, and Chinaberry wars. So, I stop by the parsonage slab once or twice a week to look for nothing in particular. Just to be there for a few minutes. And that is enough. It's not that we lived there for a long time. Just over a year, in fact. It's just that we lost so much there. The now empty lot on Washington Avenue is as close as we can be to what we lost. As close as we can get to our life before.

But to stop is also a reminder, a reminder that what is past is past. And as much as that past life is a part of me, there is much more in front of me. No matter how many beads and marbles I recover, I'll never recover the way of life that was or who I was at the time. However, if I claim that past life as a part of me now, if I remember the lessons learned, if I see the possibilities, if I seize the opportunities – life will not be as it was, it will be better.

Muddy Nose Clips

The first reminder of the hurricane that day was at the Okatoma Outdoor Post. What once was located in dense woodland was now surrounded by downed trees and cutover. A blue tarp on the roof of Ronnie and Lisa's house was another reminder. At the bridge I pulled my airbags (extra flotation in the event the boat and I get separated) out of my gear bag. They were stained with mud from Katrina. The mouthpieces, where I had to place my lips to inflate the airbags, were caked in dried mud. Another reminder of our nation's worst natural disaster. As Ben and I floated down the creek, I put my nose clips (to prevent water from going up my nose and kicking in the drowning reflex when in the upside down, low-oxygen environment) in my mouth to moisten them. I was reminded real quickly that they, too, had been immersed in muddy seawater.

All around me were reminders of the havoc wreaked by Hurricane Katrina six months before and what had begun as a sun and fun-filled escape became a day just like every other day for those of us who have

71

endured. At the first waterfall a tree lay in the rushing waters blocking our normal route through the waves and currents. Maybe a hundred yards downstream, a gigantic pine tree stretched across the creek and we had to navigate through the jungle of limbs reaching like long arms into the cold waters. Even here, in one my favorite places on earth, we were surrounded by the destruction and chaos generated by the violent winds. Is this all there is? Is there nothing else? All along our way the creek banks were cluttered with trees snapped, uprooted, and cast about like toys.

There was something else, though. Ben and I both commented along the way that we had never seen the moss on the creek banks so lush and green. Was there more moss? Was it greener? Did the open woods allow more sunshine through to enhance the contrast with the browns and grays of the dormant trees, as well as, the dead? All along the way, the green mosses and ferns were the evidence of ongoing life in the midst and prevalence of destruction and death.

At the waterfall we call "The Chute" a miracle of sorts happened. After navigating the swirling waters of "The Chute", Ben and I beached our kayaks on a sandbar for a time of rest and refreshment. While sitting on my kayak eating lunch, I glanced down and there on a twig by my leg was a cocoon. Still confused at times about what month it was, I thought it was surely too early in the year for the moth to have emerged from the warmth and mystery of the cocoon. I was surprised to find that indeed the end of the cocoon was opened. And, suddenly, so were my eyes. No longer did my vision focus on the fallen trees, the broken limbs, and the bare roots. The huckleberry bushes were in bloom. Bees buzzed, pollinating the flowers as they gathered the precious nectar. The blood-red, whirlybird maple seeds hung expectantly from twigs raised from the dead of winter. A yellow butterfly flittered through the breezes across the stream. There was life. Death did not and will not have the final say.

Once there were sporadic sunflowers emerging from the debris. Now life was bursting out all around us. Reminding us, assuring us of what we have said throughout our months of recovery, what became our mantra – "Where there is life, there is God; where there is God, there is hope."

The Birthstone Ring

Back when I was in high school, my parents surprised me one Christmas morning with a very special gift: a beautiful, yet unusual, birthstone ring. The Aquamarine stone was mounted atop a gold ring with a cluster of leaves reaching down each side of the stone. I had never seen one like nor have I seen one like it since.

Susan and I had admired it displayed in the window of Barrett's Jewelry Store. As high school sweethearts, she had wanted to surprise me with the ring, but was unable to afford the forty-dollar price. I don't know if she and my parents conspired or not. In any case, the ring became symbolic both of my parents' and Susan's love.

I wore the ring constantly. Except for bedtime I never removed it from my finger. The edges of the facets on the stone became chipped and scarred. After years of wear it got too small for my finger. I never knew gold would shrink.

Without it constantly with me, I kept it in a place of safety. In a felt pocket, in a box, in the top drawer of my dresser. Occasionally, I'd pull it out of safe-keeping, try to slip in on, and then put it back in the pocket, in the box, in the top drawer.

Neither Susan nor I can yet understand why we didn't pack more belongings, especially sentimental items like photos and jewelry, when we evacuated for Hurricane Katrina. In any case, for whatever reason, we took only the bare minimum. A few clothes. My ever-present laptop. The dogs, cats, and the metal box that contained our insurance policies. Not that they were worth anything in the end. But at the time we thought they were.

When we returned to Pascagoula on Wednesday, August 31st, we found our home destroyed and our belongings scattered with the wind. For weeks after the storm, I'd wake up in the middle of the night and in that lethargic state between oblivion and awareness remember things lost and not yet found. A Nikon camera latched safely in a water-tight case. If I could just find locate that case, maybe the camera... The Lionel train from my childhood. The collection of antique United Methodist Disciplines. The mug from which my dad had his last cup of coffee. And... one night the birthstone ring. I had to find my birthstone ring. More than anything else, I had to find that ring.

The dresser in which I kept the ring was gone from our bedroom, but a watch kept in the same drawer with the ring was found just outside the bedroom window. In all likelihood, the ring was somewhere in the room or just outside. "Miss Attention to Detail" Mandy cleaned the room all the way to the concrete slab. Earrings. Bracelets. But not my ring. We sifted through the debris in the bedroom again and again. No ring. We searched between the wall studs and the floor plate. No ring.

Outside I raked and scratched in the plants below the window. I kicked aside fragments of sheetrock and shingles. Rummaged through piles of lumber and debris. Trampled through the dead grass. No ring. Then, one day, a block away atop the remains of a house, we found the dresser.

The dresser was lying with the top drawer partially open. Navy blue socks hung over the front of the drawer. My heart nearly beat out of my chest. I approached with caution lest movement cause the ring to drop through the loose debris. I eased the drawer open and dug through the wet, muddy socks. A jewelry box with a Celtic cross from Parkway Hills was found, but not the birthstone ring. Despite a desperate search through the lumber under the dresser, there was no ring. But, there was still hope. I knew the course the water would have carried my dresser.

With the precision of a GPS I searched the suspected path the dresser would have floated from our bedroom to its final resting place. Allowing yardage to both sides of the line to allow for miscalculations or currents below the surface I scoured, I scratched, I dug. Once. Twice. Three times and more. In one direction then in reverse. No ring. My options were running out, but I knew if I found it, it would be in the last place I looked. All I had to do was find that last place to look.

The reason I reached for and opened the metal box in which our insurance papers were stashed (not that they made any difference) has been forgotten with the passage of time. When I flipped through the contents an unexpected object caught my attention. A tiny box! My heart fluttered. I opened the box. A small felt pocket. It could be safely keeping just one thing. I felt the shape through the soft material. The birthstone ring.

The ring wasn't kept where I remembered. We had taken it when we evacuated to Decatur. We had carried it back to Pascagoula. Kept it with us until we moved into our camper, the Pink Palace. That of more value than all else had been with us all along.

"Our hearts are restless until they rest in you," wrote Augustine in *Confessions*.[ii] How much money do we spend? How much energy do we expend? How many miles do we travel? How many places do we search? How many possessions must we possess? All in fruitless efforts to find what will give us the rest we seek. Yet, the restlessness persists, and the search goes on. Then one day if we search in just the right place we find the one thing of more value than all else. The One thing that will satisfy all discomforts. We find God. Then we realize, through all our quest for rest, the One who fills the void and calms the heart had been with us all along.

Katrina, Two Years Later

As I write this it is August 28. It's almost 8:30 a.m. Two years ago, August 28 was on a Sunday. At 8:30 on August 28, 2005 we were beginning our early worship service at First UMC, Pascagoula. Two years ago.

There had been a storm brewing over the previous few weeks. There was a big brouhaha over the "Hearts on Fire" conference at Lake Junaluska. Emotions ran high all across the southeast. The emotions were particularly high at Pascagoula First and the fracas reached a fever pitch on Sunday, August 21. A meeting of the Administrative Council was scheduled for August 30 to make an official response to Lake Junaluska concerning the conference.

On Sunday, August 28, when we gathered to worship, the 50 or so people attending the 8:30 service was about half our average. A storm was raging, only this storm had nothing to do with Lake Junaluska or "Hearts on Fire." Another storm was raging. This one out in the Gulf of Mexico. We had been watching it, too, for what seemed like an eternity. This storm had a name – Katrina. Once a category 5 hurricane, now diminished somewhat, but the destructive forces had already been unleashed. The category five winds, while still far out in the Gulf, had put the surge, or as we like to say, the wind-driven water on course for the coast.

I remember only a few details of the services that day. Attendance at the 11:00 service totaled about 50 as well. Those who had not evacuated were securing their homes and preparing to leave. In each service

I asked everyone to give up their usual pews and to move to the center section of the sanctuary, down front, closer to each other, closer to me. Togetherness and community were essential in the face of the storm on the horizon. More than ever, we needed each other.

I suppose my text that day would have been one of the lectionary texts. Out of curiosity I looked up those scriptures to see if I could remember which one I had chosen. I couldn't. In light of the situation it is likely I didn't preach the sermon I planned anyway.

I do remember the 8:30 children's sermon, though. I remember it because the child who was to bring the box either forgot or was not there. Whoever it was had a legitimate excuse for both. One of the parents, Alan, sneaked out of the service and returned with a box. I invited anyone to come – children and adults alike. In the box was a piece of paper, a pair of scissors, and a rock. Decisions. Decisions.

In my closet today, two years later, there is a plastic storage box. In the box are some of the sentimental things I was able to salvage from the debris left by Katrina. There is a ceramic figurine I got for my granddaddy when I went to the 1967 Boy Scout World Jamboree in Idaho. Granddaddy died in 1975. I inherited Pend Oreille Pete. I have two coffee mugs. I believe Daddy would have had his last cup of coffee at home in one of those. He was taken to the hospital with pneumonia and never went back home. He died in 2002. I inherited the mugs from the drain rack by the kitchen sink. I have a coffee cup from my grandmama's china set. We found it in a room on the other side of the house, under the carpet between the carpet pad and concrete slab – unbroken, unscratched. A miracle

I have my merit badge sash, my Eagle Scout medal, my Order of the Arrow sash, and most of the patches from my Boy Scout collection. I found the patches a quarter of a mile from our house. Spread over the mud-caked grass. Another miracle.

In a kitchen cabinet are other sentimental coffee mugs. On the bookshelves are moldy commentaries, Bibles, hymnals, and books too cherished to throw away. Throughout the house are pieces of refinished furniture – our dining table and all six chairs scavenged from our debris field, the rocking chair Susan rocked our babies to sleep in, a marble-top table held together by Gorilla Glue. Stored in the carport and displayed in the yard are rusty and corroded pieces of yard art.

Time and space won't allow me to elaborate on other miracles or memories, or the stuff we still treasure. Though not valuable in and of itself. You see, when you lose everything, anything you find is valuable, regardless of the breaks, the dents, the scratches, the rust. A watch that still runs. An antique clock that is stuck at 6:10 (a.m. on August 29). Piano hammer #41 found along Beach Blvd. A cross formed of copper wire by an unknown sculptor and embedded in the top of the cross I constructed of two by fours from our house and erected near the street.

Memories. Miracles. Valuable lessons that I hope I never forget. The most valuable lesson being: the ultimate source on which we can depend to pull us through in times of adversity is God. God who works through your family, your friends, your church, and miraculously through people and congregations you don't even know. God. And... where there is life, there is God; where there is God, there is hope.

Reflections
In
Grief

The reflections published in this section were written in the weeks and months following the deaths of my parents. My mother and father died less than three months apart in the fall and winter of 2002. Writing my thoughts and recording the emotions I felt became a part of my grief therapy as I dealt with being an orphaned adult.

Grief

Before I know it, it will have been a year since Daddy died. October 4 to be exact. He was taken to the hospital two weeks prior to his death. Pneumonia. Again. On the day of his death, we had Mama sign a power of attorney, giving us the legal authority to act in her behalf, pay bills, etc. Little did we know that in less than 3 months she would be gone from our lives as well. December 22 to be exact. She died under hospice care in my sister's home. A series of strokes. Again.

Although I knew intellectually, in my mind, that my parents were mortal, that my parents would die and although I knew that their health was failing and although I knew that they were getting on in years, in my heart I wasn't as prepared for their deaths as I thought I was. Or at least I wasn't prepared for what would happen to me when they were gone. I wasn't prepared for the sadness, the sense of loss, their absence. In short, I wasn't prepared for grief and all the emotions and feelings stirred up by grief. While I still haven't figured it all out and I still am not sure why I feel the way I do on some days, over the last several months I have been able to sort through a lot of my feelings and discern the effects that grief has had on my life and why I act just plain weird sometimes.

This discernment has not come easily, nor has it come without assistance. I have read books that have helped me understand grief better. Some of these books I have referred to others who have experienced the loss of parents. The most helpful book has been one given to me by my sister entitled <u>The Orphaned Adult</u> by Alexander Levy. As I have read Levy's book I have felt that he is telling my story and it has been a great comfort to see in writing another person's experiences that match my own. I'm not as weird as I thought I was. I'm not alone in all this. Others experience the same emotions and feelings that I have. In that fact alone, there is consolation. I'm not the only one who has ever felt this way.

I have learned through my experience, and have had affirmed through my reading, that grief is long-term, sometimes as long as two years. One does not attend the funeral, take a couple of days off from work, and then go back to life as usual. Life will never be "usual" again. I have been reminded that an active part of grief is guilt, as I have written before. I wish I had stayed with Daddy the night before he died. I wish I could have said "I love you" one more time. I wish I could have... Fill in the blanks. I have learned that grief is accompanied by depression, a sense of sadness for "no apparent reason" and disorientation. Where is my center now? Where is home? I still have longings to go home, to that house in Decatur. Look around. Smell the odors, their scents. Hope that they are still there somewhere. They're not. Where is home now?

I have discovered that apathy is tied in with grief, too. A lack of interest and enthusiasm for things once cherished, anticipated, loved. Hobbies and places of interest don't bring the same excitement or satisfaction. Relationships change. Friendships emerge, others fade. Marriages are affected. Some spouses move apart. Some grow stronger. Thankfully, mine has been the latter. There is fear arising out of the sense of my own mortality. I'm now next in line. There is no one who stands between me and death now. Life becomes more cautious, safe, protected, and less risky. Time, family time especially, takes on new and profound meaning. The only close relationships I have and on which I can hopefully depend are family: wife, children, siblings, cousins. There is a place in my heart and a longing in my life that only a mother can fill. Now there is only that, a place and a longing that no one can fill.

I have learned over the last several months that grief is strange, and no one experiences grief in the same way. Everyone grieves in his or her own unique way and the period of grief varies from one person to another. I know that there is a lot more to grief than can be summarized in a few brief paragraphs in a church newsletter. Goodness knows that all the elements of grief cannot even be contained in a single book. But, thankfully, I have been able to identify within me aspects of my grief that explain why I have felt the way I have felt for the last several months and, hopefully, will explain why I may have seemed different, distant, lethargic, and, at times, just plain weird.

Mama and Daddy's "Stuff"

I can't believe the number of pictures. Portraits. Snapshots. School pictures. More portraits. More snapshots. As we continue to sort through the stuff in Mama and Daddy's house, we find more pictures, more photos. I never knew they took so many photos or had so many portraits taken of themselves, individually and as a couple, and of the entire family. In addition to the photos there are newspaper clippings of other photos. Within the house there is an entire history of the family and separate histories of each child summed up in the photos, newspaper clippings, and other memorabilia saved over the last 60 plus years.

Over the last year we have met at Mama and Daddy's house to rummage through the stuff. I have no other word than "stuff". Rummaging and sorting the stuff. What to keep. What to sell. What to throw away. With every drawer, with every door, with every box, bag, and shelf, there is more stuff. Sorting some of the stuff is easy. Keep, sell, discard. But a lot of the sorting is difficult. Difficult because each piece of paper, each clipping, each envelope has to be opened and carefully examined, lest something of vital importance is cast away. That which is kept, then, has to be filed or boxed. Skip's stuff in his box. Rita's in hers. Kris' in his and mine in mine. There has to be a scrapbook box and keepsake box for those items that belong to us all, the family that remains. Much cannot be sold. Much cannot be thrown away.

Difficult also because with each item found, examined, and identified there is a story, a memory. Some of the sorting takes a long time because we call for each other from other rooms in the house to come and see. Then we share the memory or story of a particular item that has been found. Long lost stories are told. Long misplaced memories are shared.

Various sets of hair clippers Daddy used to cut our hair. Daddy would set us up on a stool, fasten a towel around our necks with a safety pin, and shave our heads down to a crew cut, making sure that the top was perfectly level, lest we walk around looking as if our heads were lopsided. The baby bed in which each of us slept as infants. The high chair in which we were fed as toddlers. Locks of hair from their blonde-haired daughter with a pixie cut. A blonde daughter arriving after two dark-haired sons. Beauty and the beasts. Icicles from family

Christmas trees. Each year we'd travel the dirt roads of Newton County looking for just the right cedar tree. The finishing touch was always the icicles. After Christmas, the ornaments were removed in reverse order and each icicle was carefully removed and repackaged. Fifty-nine cents after all is... fifty-nine cents.

Romance novels. Old dictionaries with crossword puzzle clues listed in the front and newspaper clippings stuffed throughout. Certificates. Homework and test papers. Science projects. Boys' Life magazines. Old farms tools that have been in the family since Daddy, Granddaddy, and our uncles owned and operated five cotton gins. When I was in the first grade I remember going by the gin in Decatur and playing in the cotton and climbing over the bales. Riding on trailer loads of cotton from the fields to the gin. Watching and waiting as a bale with fire deep inside quietly burned in Granddaddy's yard.

Posters. Paintings. Kris' artwork displayed in frames on the walls and on tabletops. With each drawer, each pile of stuff, more photos. A photograph of "The Sorce," Skip's rock and roll band in the late sixties. They played all over east Mississippi. Daddy didn't miss many of the dances for which The Sorce played. No, he didn't go to dance. Cassette tapes of almost every sermon I've preached since 1992. Newsletters with almost every article I've written.

Stuff, stuff, and more stuff. Every item carries with it a story. Every piece has a memory attached. Some good, some bad. Some pleasant, some not so pleasant. Some memories were right there on the surface of our brains. Easily remembered. Some would never have been recalled had a particular item not been saved, not been found. This is what makes the sorting so long, arduous, and, in some ways, painful. With each article a memory, with each piece a chapter in the story. What to keep, what to cast out. With each thing kept, a memory is saved. With each item sold or thrown away, a memory is lost, maybe forever.

But, we can't save it all. So, we save those dearest, those most precious and valuable, those most meaningful. Some good, some bad. Some pleasant, some not so pleasant. But memories just the same. Stories to be told and retold. Portraits of a family.

Daddy's Seeds

I don't know how long the seeds have been there. I found them in the freezing unit of one of the three refrigerators my parents had in their home. I know, most homes have only one, maybe two. But my parents were always looking for a bargain and a good deal on perishable goods usually meant buying in quantity. Extra cold space was a necessity regardless of energy costs. My parents were also gardeners. Thus, extra cold space was necessary to store freshly picked vegetables from the garden until they could be blanched, boiled, cooked, bagged, and frozen. Did I mention they also had two chest-type freezers? Two packed full of frozen veggies, picked, packed, and stored for wintertime enjoyment when the garden sat dormant, waiting for the last frost and the first seeds.

I don't know how long the seeds have been there in the freezer. What's even more puzzling is how many years of gardening they represent. In my parents' home seeds were like genes passed down from year to year. Seeds from a good crop of tasty beans, peas, and other veggies were kept and planted the following spring. So, those in the freezer today may be traced back several years, or I wouldn't be surprised to find that they could be traced back a generation or more. They may represent my first garden when I was a child. I can say with confidence they are descendants of the beans and peas my grandparents grew in the same garden plot as my dad's.

Each year my dad would take his Merry tiller and loosen the sandy soil behind my grandparents' house, which was next door to my parents', down the hill from my cousins', and just down the path from Uncle Perry's store. Each spring the soil was vigorously tilled and meticulously formed into rows. After smoothing the tops of the mounds, Daddy would carefully space out the holes, lovingly place the seeds, and then gently cover them with the sandy, fertilized soil. Then the waiting began. This was the hardest part. Waiting. Waiting for the seed to sprout. Waiting for the sprout to grow. Waiting for the blooms. Waiting for the fruit. But the waiting time was not without its work. If it was dry, the plants had to be watered. If it was wet, strategies had to be in place to drain the water from between the rows. Bean sticks had to be cut. Sweetgum saplings were the best. Holes had to be formed by jabbing a sharp-pointed, metal probe into the ground. The sticks had to be set in the holes. Then there was more waiting as the runners slowly intertwined themselves around the bean sticks. There was fertilizer to be applied to hasten the growth and stimulate fruiting. Then there was what Daddy called "laying by." I'm not sure I ever learned what that meant. Probably something akin to "I've done all I can. Sit back and wait. Let nature take its course." And it would.

Sometime in mid to late summer all the hard work would pay off. That meant, of course, more hard work. As the blooms fell off and the fruit took their place, the "ready-to-pick" vegetables had to be picked. Then shelled. Then cooked, boiled, or blanched, whatever process was called for. Once in bags or jars they were stored for winter and future enjoyment. During the peak of the growing season, not all made it to the freezer. Each meal was a feast of fresh butterbeans, fresh string beans, fresh peas, tomatoes, okra, pepper. All out of my parents' garden just outside their back door.

As the growing season waned and the time of the first frost grew near, Daddy would always leave some of the healthier beans and peas on the vines. These he would let go. Get too big and hard to eat. These he would let grow and then dry on the vines. These represented the best he had. These he would later pick and shell and store in glass jars in the freezing unit of his refrigerator. These were the seeds for the future. The seeds that would be passed on to subsequent years to be planted in ensuing gardens to provide food and fruit for the future.

Daddy hadn't gardened for the last few years. His health and the needed care for my mother following her stroke in 1998 demanded too much of his time and more energy than he had. Something had to give. As hard as it was for him to let go, gardening was his sacrifice. But, he saved the seeds. Seeds probably from the last garden he lovingly tilled, planted, harvested, enjoyed. Seeds that have now fallen into the possession of the next generation. And the next.

They're ours now. Our seeds. Entrusted to us with all the hope and dreams Mama and Daddy had for the garden each year, for the promise each seed held, for the good each seed could provide. They remain in storage, in glass jars in the freezing unit of one of their three refrigerators. I can't bring myself to throw them away. To let them go. To let them spoil. Seeds are meant to be planted. Seeds are meant to produce. To throw them away would be to deny them of their purpose, to end the cycle of life, to break a cycle began years and perhaps generations ago. They are our seeds now and it's up to us to pass on what has been passed on to us.

This spring, after the threat of the last frost, I'll take my tiller and loosen the soil in my small garden plot in my back yard. I'll form rows and add fertilizer and water. As usual, I'll plant tomatoes, okra, squash, pepper, cucumbers. My usual. But, this year I'll make a little extra room for some butterbeans and string beans. As I lovingly place the seeds in the carefully-formed holes I'll remember and give thanks. And, as the time of the first frost approaches, I'll save a few dry seeds in the freezing unit of my refrigerator. To be planted and passed on to future generations. To be planted and passed on.

Daddy's Snapper

The only thing that I know for sure is that it is a Snapper self-propelled and the engine is Briggs and Stratton. Those two facts say a lot. There are other things I know, at least, I think I know. It's old. It's dirty. It's beat up. It's tied together with bits of wire and an assortment of bolts, washers, and nuts. And... it runs... like a top! It's one of my dad's possessions that I asked to have after he and my mom died at the end of last year. I wanted it for a couple of reasons. One, I used it last summer to mow their yard. Daddy always said that he was going to mow. I guess I held out hope that he would. But years of smoking, even though he had quit some 25 years before, had paid their price. As much as he would have liked, as much as he wanted to get out and do the things he had always done, he just didn't have the breath. It had become laborious just to move about the house. Close by was his breathing treatment machine. I wanted to keep the mower probably out of the wish I had mowed the yard more often after he got where he couldn't.

I wanted to keep the mower for a second reason too. That mower says a lot about him, about the man we called Daddy. As I said, that Snapper self-propelled lawnmower is old. How old, I don't know. The serial and model numbers are visible, but that's about all. The engine, I would guess, is probably a 3 hp. The lower half of the engine is covered with grease and years of dust and grime. The upper part is covered with green algae. Algae? Yep, Daddy always kept his lawn equipment outside under makeshift shelters. Damp and shady. Just the right mix for algae to grow.

There are twists of wire that sometime in the past held something on, held something in place. I can't even bring myself to cut them lose. The side discharge doesn't match the original mower and is held on with 8-10 different combinations of bolts, washers, and nuts. None of the wheels are original. Plastic becomes brittle with age. The front wheels are transplants from another mower that finally died and gave itself up for parts. The back wheels were actually purchased, new. Not just any wheel will work on the back. While I don't know for sure, I can't imagine that the throttle cable is original nor are the drive wheels and shafts. The miracle? It runs… like a top.

Daddy was a depression era child, growing up in a time when he and his family had to "make do" with what they had. Toys were snuff bottles and other pieces of "trash" converted into a little boy's treasures. Christmas was a piece of fruit, if really lucky, a pocketknife. During the depression, everything was valuable. Everything at some time in the future could and would be used. Simplicity. Not just out of choice but out of necessity. Daddy could never throw anything away. His storage buildings are filled with bits of wire, nuts and bolts, stuff. Junk to most of us, but to him, a depression-era child, valuable resources. Simplicity. Almost anything, with a little ingenuity, can be fixed, mended, adjusted, rigged. Simplicity. Money was better saved or spent on the essentials, the necessities. And, as I remember, the kids.

Daddy grew up in a time before "planned obsolescence." Or at least in a time when he would do everything possible to save or mend before something like a lawnmower became unrepairable. Years ago, Daddy took a small engine repair course at the local community college. Not to make a living or even second income, but to keep his lawnmowers and garden tillers running. Me? If I can't get it cranked, I certainly can't fix it myself. So, I sell it at the next garage sale for ten bucks.

I brought Daddy's Snapper lawnmower home with me the other day. It hadn't been cranked since I used it last summer. I yanked on the pull cord. I yanked and adjusted the throttle cable, didn't really know which way was off or choke. I yanked and yanked. And you know what? It cranked. It still runs… like a top. In the next week or so I'm going to take it back home to Mama and Daddy's house and I'm going to mow their lawn like I did when I was a kid… like I should have done more often when they were sick. As I walk behind that old Snapper mower I'll remember the way things were and all the things there are still to learn from the man we called Daddy.

635-2187

635-2187, every time I needed advice I dialed that number. Anytime I needed comfort, anytime I needed help, anytime I just wanted to talk I dialed 635-2187. For quite some time the Decatur Telephone Directory still listed 635-2187 as the telephone number for Wilson Taylor, Decatur. The number was listed in the directory as long as I could remember. Maybe as long as there has been a Decatur Telephone Directory published. 635-2187 was the telephone number I grew up with. I guess there were a couple of other phone numbers. One when we lived for a year in Sebastopol. The "Pool" as we called it. We had a different number for the three and a half years we lived in Shady Grove, just north of Laurel where Daddy was principal. But even during those years 635-2187 was kept for our home in Decatur. That number is the phone number I remember.

For a long time, we only had one telephone, a black rotary dial phone. Way back then there were no touch tone phones, no digital systems, and in most cases only one telephone per home. Way back then the phone line was generally shared with three or four other families. A party line. Each party had their own "ring" – one ring, two rings, three short rings. If you answered following a ring that wasn't yours, you answered another party's call. It wasn't unusual to pick up the phone to make a call and to interrupt an ongoing conversation. Long-winded phone calls were not tolerated. They tied up the phone for all the families on the party line.

When I was in the tenth grade there was this new girl in town I met in Sunday school at Decatur Methodist Church. She had moved to town with her parents while I was on a Boy Scout trip to the World Jamboree. 1967. I took a liking to this new girl in town. I remember one day Daddy was turning the crank on the ice cream freezer making home-made ice cream. He asked me if there was any particular girl in town I was interested in. I mentioned the new girl in town. He wasn't surprised. I sat at the table in near panic and used the phone connected to 635-2187 to call her, to ask her out. I don't know how many times I put the receiver down or I hung up before she answered. She was the first girl I had ever asked out on a date. Her name was Susan. We married in December 1973.

635-2187 was the phone number my buddies knew. Over that land line we called practice for our band, "The Beginnings End." Over that phone we finalized plans for Boy Scout campouts, road trips to haunted houses, rounds of golf, games of pool (at our house, not the pool hall). 635-2187 was as much a part of growing up as anything.

When I moved away to Mississippi State, then to Jackson; when I moved to Atlanta, then to Adams UMC; when I moved to Madison, 635-2187 was my link back home. Rather than dialing FROM that number, I dialed TO that number. There were voices on the other end I wanted to hear. Advice I needed, promises of help, words of comfort. 635-2187. Sometimes, there would be Mama's voice. Sometimes Daddy's. After Mama had a stroke in 1998, she rarely answered. When she did, it was a real treat. Almost always Daddy answered, and I'd say "Hey" and he'd always reply, "Hey, yourself." It became the customary beginning to our conversation that usually addressed no topic of real importance, only a conversation for the purpose of hearing each other's voice, knowing everybody was okay, everything was the same as the last time we talked, everything was right with our world. Every conversation ending with "I love you."

Even now I have the urge, the strong desire to pick up my telephone, touch tone, digital, and one of several in my house and dial 635-2187. Nowadays, I want to dial that number and I want Daddy to pick up on the other end. "Hey," I'd say. And he'd answer, "Hey, yourself." And we'd talk just like we always did. But now when I dial there's no answer. The phone rings and rings. No one picks up. In the past I'd wonder where Mama and Daddy were, why they didn't answer. Now when no one answers, I know why. Nobody's home… anymore.

I had to give up P.O. Box 26. I had to give up the post office box that had been my grandparents' up until their deaths and then my parents'. I had to give it up in order for mail to be forwarded to my home address. I couldn't give up 635-2187 easily, though. There were just too many memories connected to that line. But, I had to give it up eventually and the end of an era, a generation had come. Yes, it was sad, hard to do, but such is the nature of life. Passing the torch. Handing off the baton. Life and death. Beginnings and endings. Saying "hello." Saying "goodbye."

Going Home

I hadn't been back in a couple of weeks. Doesn't sound like a long time and the calendar says it wasn't. But something inside of me felt it had been too long. I needed to go. Most of the times that I have returned to my home town and the surrounding area have been to do the business of executing the will. Combining assets. Filing papers. Closing accounts. Paying bills. Etc. Etc. Each time I go I stop by my parents' house to make sure everything is okay. Just to check, you know.

I hadn't been back in a couple of weeks and something inside of me felt it had been too long. There was the feeling of guilt, guilt for not having been back. But there was something else as well. A sadness. A loneliness. An absence. I know these emotions and feelings are understandable. Nobody expects me to feel otherwise. I mean, you lose two people who have been a part of your life for... your whole life; it would be odd to feel otherwise. The two people who had always been there... constancy, security, identity. The two who had given me life to begin with, cared for me, loved me, gave themselves for me. Two people over a period of three months suddenly... gone. Gone physically from my life forever. I had to go back. At least for a little while.

I went on a Friday. I went to the house in which my mother and my dad lived for close to 60 years. Almost their whole married life they lived in that house. A house in which they created a home. Reared their kids. Celebrated Christmases, birthdays, anniversaries. Hosted friends and neighbors. But nothing was better than welcoming their children home. They were the ones we returned to. It was the place we returned to. There we remembered who we were and whose we were.

I had to go back because it is the one place I can go and be as close to them as is humanly possible. Entering their house the smells engulf me and carry me back. I can see the Christmas tree laden with icicles and colored lights, supported by the piles of gifts underneath. I can see the dining table filled with fried chicken, turnip greens, cornbread, butterbeans. All steaming hot. I can see us packed around the table. Daddy on one end. Mama on the other, ready to streak to the kitchen to refill tea glasses or get the dessert. I can see us out on the concrete slab (the patio, for the city slickers) Daddy turning the crank on the ice cream freezer. I can see the beds in which they slept and the couch on which Daddy sat as he worked the daily crossword puzzle. The dinette in which breakfast was eaten, but only after Daddy had read the daily devotion from the <u>Upper Room</u>. Mama's homemade biscuits and cane syrup. Hot coffee – Luzianne with chicory (It'd put hair on your chest.). So many memories. As close to them as I can be now that they're gone.

I had to go. Go home. It's there that I remember who they were. Their love. Their sacrifices. I guess we thought they'd always be there. It would have been great, but we knew deep down inside they wouldn't and now they're gone. In their absence and in my loneliness, I go to the place where the most of who they were still is. Home. Because in a way they are still there. In the smell of the house. In the memories. In the dishes that remain in the dish drainer. In the clothes that remain stacked in piles. In the toiletries that remain in the bathrooms. In the medicine that remains in newly opened packages. Just like they've gone for the day to visit family and friends in Noxapater or Nanih Waiya or Laurel. Or out for a ride in the country. But they won't be back.

I had to go. I felt better for having gone. Yes, it was sad, real sad. But it helped. I was with them, at least in spirit, for just a little while. I cried and as I left I said goodbye. It was hard, always will be. But, it's good to have a place to go.

One Year Later

Just a feeling. Or a sensation. Or a mood. These are the only words I can come up with to describe what I was experiencing. I don't know that these words actually describe the emotion. I just had a "feeling" that something was not right. Hollowness. Emptiness. A "feeling" that something was missing. A void or chasm down deep within my being. I don't know what triggered the "feeling." Maybe it was the hint of autumn in the air. Cooler temperatures. Lower humidity. Maybe it was the October blue skies that unfurled overhead early in the month of September. Maybe it was the subtle changes in the leaves, in the weather, in the season. Maybe it was all of the above that bred the feeling of inner sadness. Reminders of a time of utter grief.

Then, I remembered. Then, I knew. It was one year ago. I was in North Carolina when I got the call from my sister that she had taken Daddy to the hospital with pneumonia and my Mama to a hospice for the care she needed. One year ago, that Daddy's last two weeks on this earth was spent in a Meridian hospital shaking uncontrollably, gasping for breath, being poked, probed, pricked, and prodded. One year ago, that Daddy lay in the hospital bed... dying. One year ago, that I fed him his food; sat at his bedside, told him I loved him... for the last time. One year ago, this Saturday, he died. No more talk of family history, gardening, or politics (although I had learned to stay away from that topic). No longer stretched out on the couch working the daily crossword puzzle. No more hugs. No more "I love you." One year ago. My, how time flies.

We were in North Carolina last week, Susan and me. Funny how history repeats itself. This time, no emergency phone calls. Just the uncanny feeling, remembering, reliving. Grief is a funny thing. On Sunday, we swung by Decatur to pick up Mimi who had spent the week in her home while we were away. Before leaving town, I had to go by the cemetery. I had to go, not because there was anything I had to do there. I just had to go. You understand. I pulled a few weeds that the caretaker had missed. Smoothed out the sand. Brushed dust and grass clippings off the cold granite markers with the dates engraved, October 4, 2002 and December 22, 2002. It was the only care I can now give. One year later.

I sent Susan and Mimi on toward Madison. I wanted to stop by Mama and Daddy's house before I followed. The lawn is uncut, and a large limb has fallen in the backyard. The house is damp, and spiders are starting to spin their webs. The house is cluttered with bags and boxes from our initial attempts to sort through a lifetime. Beyond the musky smell of a house unlived in, there are still the familiar smells. One of the reasons I go, in fact is to sense the smells. Their smells. And in a least a small way be close to them.

The den has changed. The couch on which Daddy worked the crossword puzzles is gone, as is most of the other den furniture. In their bedroom their beds are still made, and I stroked the sheets on which they last slept. In the kitchen the dishes are still in the drainer, just as Daddy left them the day Rita carried him to the hospital, one year ago. I felt the plates and lifted the old butcher knife that has been around as long as I can remember. I guess Daddy washed the breakfast dishes that morning and I remembered the cup from which he would have had his morning coffee. One year ago. And I cried.

When I walked out the front door, I was overcome by the memories of having left out that door so many times before. Was it the late afternoon sun? Was it the blue sky and cool breeze? Was it the smell of the St. Augustine grass I had mowed as a youngster? It was if I was leaving just as I had in the past. Mama and Daddy sitting in the swing and lawn chairs. Or since her stroke in 1998, Daddy having rolled Mama to the front door in her wheelchair. Mama sitting; Daddy standing behind. Waving. One last chance to say goodbye.

As I pulled out of their driveway and onto the highway, I was moved to blow the horn. We always did. Every time we left them, the last act was to blow the horn. One more way to say goodbye. You understand. On Sunday, I blew the horn and looked back expecting to see Mama and daddy seated in the swing or standing in the door in the late afternoon autumn sun. But they weren't there. And, except in my mind and in my heart, they never will be again. My, how time flies.

The Liturgy of the Earth

Seasons

Well, it's finally here. For some it seems like it took forever to arrive. For others, it seems like it occurred overnight. The calendar says it arrived on Saturday, March 20. Sometime in the early morning hours, the path of the sun passed over the equator and began its journey north toward the Tropic of Cancer. Although it seemed to come earlier this year, calendar-wise, that is, spring had begun. Officially, spring has sprung. Everything is born anew, everything is alive once more.

The evidence of spring's arrival is all around us. I look for the bluets first, poking their delicate, daisy-like, bright blue heads up through the still-brown grass. They are, for me, the first true sign of spring. Vacant lots turn a sea of pastel pink as the spring beauties paint the landscape. Pastures glow a yellow brighter than the sun, flooded by thousands of wild buttercups. Wildflowers, weeds to some, with their colors, both subtle and dazzling, coat the countryside. Early spring shrubs, colors dabbled here and there, dot our manicured lawns. A myriad of colors replaces the dull grays and browns of winter. All over the fields, there is life.

Leaves burst forth from tree limbs, emerging and starting their internal engines to produce food to sustain the life to the tree. Buds, lying beneath protective scales all winter, emerge and burst forth in their complete radiance. Bare limbs become decorated with shades of green and adorned with intermingled flowers like ornaments on a Christmas tree. Throughout the forests, there is life.

Winter. Spring. Summer. Fall. The seasons of the year. The cycle of life. That which was dead is born again. That which is born grows and produces fruit, gives birth. That which gives birth, matures, then ages, grows older. As it does it finds usefulness in providing shelter, shade, protection, home. As winter approaches and the air turns cool, daylight shortens; the sun remains low in the sky. The greens and the brilliance of summer are transformed. Colors again paint the landscape. But these colors rather than signaling the beginning of something new, something alive, are a prelude to death. Again, the colors are short-lived. As the winds turn violent and cold from the north, the last evidence of life reluctantly releases its grip and floats with resignation to the ground. The cycle of life.

But all is not lost. All is not as it appears. Death does not have the last say. Beneath the fallen leaves, protected in a blanket of warmth and darkness, life is still at work. The seeds from last spring's bloom-ing and last summer's fruits lie waiting, waiting for that magical time when the sun shines high in the sky, the wind blows from the south and the air warms. Suddenly for some yet gradually for others, the wild-flowers thrust their dainty, colored heads up through the rot and decay and once again there is life.

The bare and barren limbs, appearing dead to all, are yet alive. They, too, are just waiting. Waiting for the right time when the sap rises, the water of life flows again through the veins. Buds burst. Leaves emerge. The process repeats and once again there is life.

The seasons of the year. The seasons of life. The cycle of life. From the dead comes life. Life will end in death. But death will not win in the end. Christ has seen to that. For even in death, there is life. Death leads to life. Through baptism we die, and we rise. Death and life. Dead to our former selves and life anew in Christ. When we pro-fess faith in Christ, when we say to God and the world "I want to be a Christian," we die and rise. We say goodbye to the people we were, and we greet the new. "If anyone is in Christ, there is a new creation: everything old has passed away; see, everything has become new." (2 Corinthians 5:17) We die and rise. Death and life. "I came that they may have life," says Jesus. (John 10:10) But, before there can be life, there is death. Out with the old. In with the new.

When we come to the end of our days, the promises stand true again. In death, there is life. "Unless a grain of wheat falls into the earth and dies, it remains just a single grain; but if it dies, it bears much fruit." (John 12:24) Out of death comes life. Death does not, will not, have the last word. Life wins.

Winter. Spring. Summer. Fall. The seasons of the year. From death to life. The seasons of life. There can be life, true life, real life, eternal life, but first something must die.

A Tallahatchie Spring

It took barely a week for the world to fervently begin a complete transformation. Whether you're walking in the Park by the River, bicycling the quiet New Albany streets, or cruising the roads of Union County, it's impossible to miss evidence of the transformation. Fields have taken on the deep purple hue. Roadsides appear as a seascape of rose and pink. Lawns a glaze of lavender, pink, or a diffusive blend of spring pastels. The earth all around transformed from the earth tones of winter to the stunning and picturesque landscape no human mind could imagine, no human hand create, no human artist completely replicate.

The world was not so just over a week ago. Oh, here in New Albany it was in its earliest stages of change. When I took a trip to central Mississippi a couple of weeks ago I watched the change become more obvious as I traveled farther south. I saw my first patch of bluets just outside the Decatur city limits on the old Tommy Cumberland place. That telltale patch of lavender. For me, a sentimental, yet accurate sign of the imminence of spring and the immanence of God.

All along Highway 15 on my return trip to New Albany on Friday I gazed at the passing countryside, surveying the landscape to determine just how far north I could locate that revealing sign of lavender. Philadelphia. Louisville. Mathiston, Houston, and Pontotoc. Spring was moving north. Then back here at home, to my surprise, bluets!! Spring!! Life goes on!! Everything but the calendar said, "Spring!"

Then came Saturday morning. March 8. Snow! The earth lay covered under a cold blanket of snow. The daffodils that marked the old home places nodded, as if burdened by sadness, under the weight of the snow. The chimes of the yellow bells were muffled by the covering of white. And the bluets? Those dainty flowers on their spindly stalks? Smothered under the icy shroud of winter. I had been deceived. Spring had not sprung. Life had not returned. Death still held its grip. I had been deceived. Or… so I thought.

In Mississippi, most snows are short-lived. By that Saturday afternoon, where the sun's brightness warmed the earth, the snow retreated. And as Susan and I rode along old Highway 78, the snow had retreated to reveal a lavender lawn, a perfusion of bluets, standing straight and strong. Daffodils stood tall and proud guarding old home places. The chimes of the forsythia bells rang clearly in the cold, clear air. The only deception was to think that life could be defeated. That death still held its sting. I had been deceived. Beneath the carpet of ice, life prevailed. Though hidden from view, God was at work. The transformation of the world was underway.

Today the transformation continues. The hand of the divine Sower has strewn the seeds of life with reckless abandon and, all around, the world is reborn. On Moss Hill Dr. or Glendale Road. Along Bankhead, Central, or Hillcrest. In North Haven, Ingomar, Myrtle, East Union or West. The evidence is indisputable. Bluets. Spring Beauties. Henbit. Johnnie Jump Ups. Daffodils, flowering quince, and forsythia. Just to name a few. The hand of God has painted our landscape with the colors of life. Death has been defeated. Nothing can hinder the movement of God.

According to Matthew's Gospel, after the burial of Jesus the guards, concerned that the government officials may be duped by the disciples, went to Pilate and asked for permission to add additional security precautions at the grave. With conviction, with doubt, or with what could have been a touch of skepticism Pilate replied, "Go, make it as secure as you can." (Matthew 27:65) Perhaps even Pilate knew the impossible task of standing in the way of God.

Behind the giant stone, God's hand was at work. A miracle was in the works. The world was about to be transformed. In the end no stone was heavy enough. No seal strong enough. No guard of soldiers brave enough. Death would not win. Life would prevail. On Sunday morning, in the garden ablaze in the colors of life, the stone was rolled aside. The tomb was empty! Christ has risen! Christ has risen, indeed! Nothing would ever be the same again.

Chelsea

For the most part I like flexibility, variety, and change. Except for a few cases I don't like schedules, structure, or inflexibility. Routine is monotonous to me, boring, unexciting. When I was teaching school, I loved the students. I loved the subjects that I taught. I loved academia. I hated the everyday routine. In a life arranged, structured, routine, I slip into a rut. But, even my life, built around variety and flexibility, contains some routine. I like structure and consistency in worship. I like organization and planning in programs. Planning and structure, but always with an element of variety and flexibility. It's just who I am, my personality. Others are different, even opposite of me.

My favorite routine is the early morning. I enjoy getting up early. Making a pot of coffee and retrieving my newspaper from the driveway. I relax sitting in the recliner or on the end of the sofa with the paper and a good cup of coffee. The early mornings are my time – my time to relax, read, meditate, write, move real slow. But the early mornings are not mine anymore. My routine has been disrupted. Activity, disruption, and chaos reigns supreme.

Chaos has come to my mornings in the form of an 8-pound bundle of energy named Chelsea. Chelsea is a 2-month old Pembroke Welsh Corgi. She has been with us for just over 2 weeks now. We were warned. Yes, adequately warned. Warned in the book on Corgis we bought. Warned by the breeder in Flora. Warned by the vet. Corgis are active dogs, especially when puppies. They need, seek, and demand attention. The book says if they are not entertained, they'll find something to entertain themselves with. My experience so far is that they'll entertain themselves with dead bugs, potted plants, socks, and electrical cords. Anything else lying around is open game. We've had to baby proof our house all over again.

Corgis are herding dogs, so they like to nip at your heels as you walk. They like for everyone to be together in one room and they'll try to herd everyone, especially children, to the one room. They'll tug on shirt sleeves and pants. In the absence of protective clothing they'll tug on hands, arms, toes, and ankles. Still longing for her mom and nourishment, ears are an attractive target. My arms and hands look like I've been through a briar patch.

Our den floor is covered with toys. Looks like when Mandy and Ben were infants and toddlers. We've spared no expense to entertain and occupy the attention of this whirlwind of activity, disorder, and pandemonium. There is a toilet paper roll and a paper towel roll. There is a tissue of fabric softener, snatched from a pile of clothes just removed from the dryer. A gold bow plucked from a potted plant given to Susan during the holidays. A paper wad. She has a basket with store-bought toys – balls, a fake bone, stuffed animals, a long, elastic elephant for games of tug-of-war. Winnie gave her a dog house and a chair. Parenthood all over again. If I had forgotten what it was like and failed to empathize with parents of very young children, I'm sorry. Now I remember. My thoughts and prayers are with you.

All this and I have failed to report on progress made in potty-training, house-breaking as it is called in the pet realm. Let me just say this, dogs have to go, rain or shine, hot or cold, day or night. It makes no difference to them. We keep old shoes, a towel, and an umbrella by the door with the leash. We have to stay prepared and alert. At nine weeks, Chelsea's urges are frequent, her muscles untrained, her patience short, and her feet quick.

As I write this, Chelsea is in her kennel. I'm holed up in my study, part of my Tuesday morning routine. I try to start writing my newsletter article at 7:30 a.m. so I can email it to Angel at the office by nine. Remember, I have to have some routine. Between 5:30 and 7:30 I tried to wear Chelsea down, so I could have my hour and a half of peace and quiet to write. Peace and quiet have become commodities, bought at a high price. So far so good, but peace and quiet are also temporary, around here at least.

People are prone to ask why we would get a puppy if she creates this much trouble. Or why would we get another pet when we already have pets. Why? In short, fun. For all she demands, when it comes down to it, she's just plain fun to have around. In addition, for all she demands, there is so much more that she gives. What she gives she doesn't give back or in return - something that it would be good for all of us to learn. She just gives. Pets, especially dogs, are the epitome of unconditional love.

Our household is far from routine now. Maybe we needed that, too. To have something new, challenging. To have something that would provide laughter and joy. Something that would jar us out of our rut and routine. Something that would make us look at life in a new way. Again, something that maybe all of us need in one way or another. A little chaos to shake up our lives. Disruptions in the order of our day to remind us we can't and don't control everything. Maybe we all need something to excite us, incite us. An intrusion into our routine and structured lives. Like Easter.

Easter

Time was the day was just an ordinary day. The first day of the week. Back to work. Raising a family. Making a living. Doing what comes naturally. Ordinary. Commonplace. Routine. Everyday. Sunday. Then one Sunday, the third day after Friday, God changed the routine, the commonplace, the everyday. God transformed the first day of the week from ordinary to extraordinary. "…you are looking for Jesus of Nazareth, who was crucified. He has been raised; he is not here." (Mark 16:6) Christ is risen! Christ is risen, indeed! Resurrection. Easter. And Sunday, the first day of the week, became a day of worship. Every Sunday an Easter.

We knew something was special about this past Sunday. Not because of our local newspaper, this made no reference to the extraordinariness of the day. No "Happy Easter!" on the front page. Not because of the local businesses, they carried on business as usual. Cash registers ringing. But, we knew something was different. We knew Sunday was out of the ordinary because Easter is what we as the Christian church are all about. Easter makes us different from any other institution, any other organization, any other religion, any business, any group, any society. On Sunday morning many congregations gathered at sunrise outside to worship. That's unique. At their usual times, for some churches at additional times, congregations packed into worship services like large cans of sardines. That's incredible. Naves adorned with Easter lilies. Chancels aglow with candles. Altars draped in white. Choirs sang glorious anthems and magnificent renditions of Handel's "Hallelujah Chorus." Preachers preached with fire about new life, second chances, transformation. Drama. Emotion. Power. There had to be something extraordinary about the day. There was something in the air. Something out of the ordinary about this day. Something that made it different from all other Sundays. It was Easter. The day. THE day. Christ is risen! Christ is risen indeed!

Then, Monday. The second day of the week. The day we in the 21st century go back to work. Raising a family. Making a living. Doing what comes naturally. Ordinary. Commonplace. Routine. Everyday. Monday. All holidays are over, gone, and done with. Now it is truly back to normal. The local newspaper headlines cover the war in Iraq winding down and a nation trying to get back to business as unusual. A man in California has been arrested for the death of his wife and unborn son, already named Conner. A fire ripped through a Ridgeland apartment complex and left families without. A new epidemic rages through Asia and results in the cancellation of holiday celebrations. The Israeli – Palestinian conflict continues. Our economy is shaky at best. Iran. Syria. North Korea. Not to mention warring factions in almost every corner of the globe. Yep, Monday. Business as usual. We are so accustomed to it that we are almost blind to it. Ordinary. Commonplace. Routine.

Did Sunday make any difference at all? Did Easter make any difference? It's not just a matter of hostilities abroad. There are troubles at home, too. In our homes. In our offices. Where we work, live, and play. Distraught parents. Confused children. Angry spouses. Misplaced priorities. Powerplays to get one up, to get ahead. What goes around, comes around. Did Sunday make any difference at all? Time will tell. But if experience is any teacher, it probably didn't in most people. Why else would the Sunday after Easter become known as "low Sunday?" Not because of low emotions. But, because it is the Sunday with the lowest average worship attendance of the whole year.

Did Easter make any difference? Was God's gift to us worth it? Was Jesus' sacrifice of any significance to us? Did it transform us? The proof is in the pudding. The evidence is in the everyday, the commonplace, the routine. If Easter makes any difference it will be shown in our ordinary, daily lives.

The Colors of Life

As I look down through the woods on a mid-October morning, the mist from the over-night rain still drifts with the breeze. The woods are silent except for the occasional cry of the rain crow from the tree tops. The woods are tranquil, nothing moves. As of everything stands silently and reverently in awe of the vibrant colors of a Smoky Mountain autumn.

Even if I were an accomplished artist, I don't think I would ever imagine painting the blend of colors and the variation in hues. If I could capture on film or canvas the vibrancy of colors as accurately as they are displayed before me, no one would believe they were actually observed in the real world. No one would ever consider blending such colors together in one scene. No one except the Master Painter, the Master Artist. Not just reds. Not just yellows. Not just greens. More hues than the colors of the rainbow. Colors I can't even name to distinguish one from another. But, there they are, in all their dazzling grandeur and brilliant splendor.

Of course, similar scenes are admired throughout creation. God doesn't limit his creativity and imagination to the autumn woodlands and mountainsides. God's paint brush strokes the unimaginable colors of a sunset. God's artistic hand moves across the surface of the ocean. His endless palette of colors dapples the landscape in spring. God's creativeness and inspiration touches every aspect of the world in which we live and have our being.

In Genesis, there is the incredible story of the creation of the cosmos. A litany of praise for the Creator. "In the beginning God…" (Genesis 1:1) Out of chaos and confusion God began to shape the world as we know it. Heavens and earth. Land and water. Plants. Animals. Humans. Each more diverse than the human mind can conceive. "And God saw everything that he had made, and indeed, it was very good." (Genesis 1:31)

I was taken back recently to the story of Noah and the ark a little later in Genesis. What struck me in this instance was not the ark or the flood or the destruction of sinful humanity. Instead, I was reminded that after the destruction God recreated what he had made the first time. Again, newness came out of destruction and chaos. The insight I had, though, was the mind-boggling assortment of creatures. We are accustomed to cows, horses, dogs, cats, deer, rabbits, squirrels, and such. In their familiarity to us, they somewhat lose their uniqueness. Ever thought about a giraffe? An elephant? A platypus? How about a kangaroo? A newt, frog, snake, or spider? Paramecium, amoeba? Again, the diversity is amazing, and it exceeds my ability to describe and identify. "And God saw everything that he had made, and indeed, it was very good."

Go to a theme park sometime. Six Flags Over Somewhere. Disney World and Epcot. If you can't go that far, try the state fair. Or on the local level, just go to Walmart. Look around. There is no one just like you. With all the people in the whole-wide world, there is nobody just like you. Or me. An assortment of races, creeds, colors, language, and nationalities. "Jesus loves the little children, all the children of the world. Red and yellow, black and white, they are precious in his sight.

Jesus loves the little children of the world." There are all those colors again. "And God saw everything that he had made, and it was very good."

No wonder someone coined the phrase, "Variety is the spice of life." Think how boring life would be if every plant and animal were identical. How mundane our existence if there were no shades of the primary colors. How humdrum our days would be if God had limited his creativity with the humans who populate the earth and every sixth person looked just like you. Or worse, like me.

There is no doubt that unexpected assortments, unimaginable variations, and miraculous blends are at the heart of God and God's creativity. God loves diversity. In God's mind, variety must be the spice of life. Let's celebrate life!! In all its wonder-full diversity!

The Circle of Life

The leaves were already starting to fall. Although it was only mid-September, autumn was in the air in the mountains of North Carolina. Early one morning while everyone else was asleep I sat and watched as the leaves began to let go of their grasp and drift uncomplainingly to the moist ground below. Their work was for the summer was done. The circle of life.

Throughout the warm, sunny days of the mountain summer, the leaves had gathered water collected by the roots, breathed in carbon dioxide from the air, and utilizing a chemical reaction fueled by the energy of the sun had processed the food necessary to sustain the growth of the plant. Through the veggies and meats that we eat, the same food produced by the leaves and stored in the plant's tubs and vats sustains us and provides the necessary energy to work and play. The circle of life.

Most of us had just as soon forget all that biology stuff. Photosynthesis. Chemical reactions. Carbon dioxide plus water in the presence of chlorophyll and utilizing the sun's energy yields sugar and oxygen. Oxygen? The waste product of photosynthesis, oxygen, necessary for all animal life, is dumped back into the atmosphere. Inhaled as we breathe. Giving us life. Sustaining our life. And every time we exhale our breath dumps carbon dioxide into the air. A waste product of

106

respiration. Inhaled by the plants. Giving them life. The process begins again. The circle of life.

As I sat there early on that mountain morning while the others slept I reflected on the leaves as they drifted to their earthly resting place. The interconnectedness of all living things. Dependence. Without green plants, without leaves and the miracle of photosynthesis, there wouldn't be enough oxygen to support animal life on earth… human life on earth. A living organism, as ordinary as a plant and sometimes pesky enough that we cut, prune, chop, and trim, provides the very element necessary for human life. In return, we provide the necessary compounds to complete the cycle. Without the plants the carbon dioxide would build up in the atmosphere and human life would cease, suffocated by our own breath. Reliance. Interdependence. Plants and animals utilizing the waste products of the other to grow and produce. We are not truly independent nor are we ever truly free. The circle of life.

With each passing breeze another leaf would resign itself to its destiny and quietly let go of its hold and float gently to the earth below, their summer work done. The circle of life. But, no, the circle is not yet complete. There on the forest floor something else is happening. Other changes take place. The once green leaf, now brown, begins to rot and decay. Giving nutrients back to the soil. Giving life back to the plant that gave it life. Even in its death and decay the leaf continues to give life. Ashes to ashes. Dust to dust. And in the spring the plant will draw those nutrients into itself, the tips of the branches will bud, and new leaves will burst forth. And the cycle will continue. Even in death, there is life. The circle of life.

Remember and Give Thanks

Clear, crisp autumn days. Newly fallen leaves and pine straw covering the ground. The smell of Thanksgiving dinner being prepared in the kitchen. I remember the whole family, everybody, gathering at Grandmama and Granddaddy Taylor's house. I remember sitting down to Thanksgiving dinner, only a few able to sit at the dining room table. Everyone else scattered wherever there was room to sit. I don't remember turkey, but I remember fried chicken. I remember cornbread dressing, gibblet gravy, fresh-out-of-the-garden turnip greens, recently "put up" butterbeans and string beans, coconut cake, peanut brittle, pecan pies. A feast. A Thanksgiving feast. As good as the food was it was made even better by the fact that the whole family was together – for at least one more time.

I remember the Cowboys – Lions game on the TV in the den. I remember our own football game played out in Grandmama and Granddaddy's front yard. The goal line on one end was the redbud bush, on the other end the sewage ditch – hopefully cleared in one long leap. Some of us made it, some fell short, some fell in. If you fell in, you weren't tackled the rest of the game. I remember all the grandsons going squirrel hunting in the afternoon. Shaking vines and scaring the living daylights out of the squirrels. Back then squirrels were good eating when fried crisp and served with homemade biscuits and gravy. However, more squirrels got away than got put in our game pouches.

Probably my fondest memory was the annual trip to the Addy farm out in the country where, each Thanksgiving, they cooked cane syrup. It was like a trip back in time, to a simpler time, a less complicated time when families subsisted on their fortitude, creativity, ingenuity, and faith. As the old mule made countless rounds turning the cane mill, the juice flowed into the cooker where it was cooked down into rich, thick syrup. Hanging next to the spigot that controlled the flow of juice into the cooker was an old aluminum cup. Daddy would always take the cup and fill it with the fresh juice and drink it like tea. I preferred chewing the tough, stringy cane. Daddy always carried home some of the syrup, still warm in the can.

Regardless of the daily activities and events, at the core of our gathering was what we knew was the real purpose of the day – thanks giving, giving thanks. Remembrance. Remembering that we were family and that we didn't face the trials, tribulations, and troubles of life alone. Around the over-burdened table, we remembered the bounty we enjoyed and, while we didn't have everything we wanted, we had everything we needed. The Thanksgiving meal was always preceded, as was every meal in our homes, with the blessing. "Percy, say the blessing." "Heavenly Father, accept our thanks for these and all our blessings." I don't know where the prayer came from. I just remember Granddaddy saying it before each meal. Then Daddy like his daddy. Then I, as them. Passed down from generation to generation. Like a thread carefully woven into the fabric a warm comfortable sweater. A prayer that served to remind us and express our thanks. Remembrance.

Remembrance that all our blessings are a gift, a gift from God. All that we have comes from the Source of all things. All that we are comes from the Spring of life. Remembrance – giving thanks for the blessings of life. Not that we had everything we wanted but we had everything we needed. Not that everything worked out the way we had hoped, but that through God's never-ending grace and abiding love everything worked out for the best.

We each have our memories. Many of us share similar if not the same memories. That's what Thanksgiving is all about. Reunion. Acknowledging our dependence on each other – we are not alone. Remembrance. What we are, what we have is a gift from God. Giving thanks for the blessings of life. "Heavenly Father, accept our thanks..."

Christmas Promises

"I'm dreaming of a white Christmas, just like the ones I used to know." "Sleigh bells ring, are you listening? In the lane snow is glistening. ...walking in a winter wonderland." "Jingle bells, jingle bells, jingle all the way. O what fun it is to ride in a one-horse open sleigh." I have dreamed of a white Christmas, but I've never actually awakened on Christmas morning to newly (or previously) fallen snow. We came within two days one time, in *south* Mississippi, no less. I've never heard sleigh bells ring much less ridden in a sleigh pulled by one (or more) horses. I've been sold a bill of goods. Songs, cards, television specials all romanticize Christmas and promise me a Christmas I've never experienced. In fact, unless one lives way "up north" or travels to the mountains or northern climes, the chances of experiencing a white Christmas is extremely small. Just ask the Weather Channel. They make the predictions. Will my dreams of a white Christmas come true?

"Rudolph the Red-Nosed Reindeer". Now, there's a Christmas song that has it right. I can relate to a foggy Christmas Eve. I can relate to a Caribbean Christmas, temps in the 70's and 80's. More like time to go to the beach than something as alien as snow skiing or snowboarding. I can relate to a rainy Christmas, a hot, humid Christmas, a cool Christmas, and an occasional clear Christmas. Just once I'd like to see all those promises of a white Christmas come true. Until then I'll keep creating one of my own. Lighted imitation icicles hang from the eve of my roof. A little fake snow and frost sprayed on the window panes. Cotton balls carefully placed around the base of the tree take on a "snow-like" appearance and feel like it if we can turn the air conditioner down low enough. If we get the house cold with the AC we can even build a fire in the fireplace. Of course, now we just turn on the gas. The logs are fake, too. But they do look real especially with the fake coals. Voila!! My very own "white" Christmas.

There have been other "Christmas" promises, as well. Usually originating with poets and painters and retailers and merchandisers. Excuse my cynicism. What about "Peace on Earth?" Wasn't that a promise of Christmas? Didn't we hear that from the prophets of old? The angels who spoke to the shepherds as they kept watch over their flocks by night? Didn't the coming of the Messiah promise peace of earth? Where is it? For 2000 years people have been killing people. Today, there are wars and rumors of wars. Violence. Terrorism. Murders and killings. There's no peace on earth. Of course, we can explain that. The prophets and angels were just talking about spiritual peace. Not peace among people, not peace among nations.

And... What about good will among men (politically correct read "people")? That was a promise made, too. The angels sang it with all the heavenly hosts. Instead we have bitterness, hatred, anger, jealousy, envy, strife. Just human emotions we say. Just part of our humanity. Excuses. Sounds like we've been sold another bill of goods.

But... wait. Christmas is not just pretty scenes painted on the fronts of cards. Christmas is not just sentimental musical favorites. Christmas is more than trees and lights and presents and snow. Look closely at the manger scene over there. See in the manger there is a baby. Wrapped warmly and lovingly in bundles of torn cloth. Eyes wide open with wonder. In the manger, there is a baby. But there is something else there too. There's more. As the starlight filters through the cracks of the drafty stable, a shadow is cast across the delicate newborn baby. The shadow is ominous, almost seems out of place. And, if you look carefully, you can see that it is the shadow of a cross.

The baby is not just any baby. The child born is not just any child. This is Jesus. Jesus the Christ. The Messiah. Not in the usual sense of the word. Not as expected down through the ages. By means of this Child the law will be written on the hearts of people, not sheets of paper. Because of this Child lives will be changed, hearts will be transformed. Peace on earth will come. Good will among all people will happen. But only when we decide for it to be so.

The promises of Christmas are just empty promises, pie in the sky in the sweet by and by, until we decide the promises of Christmas are as real today as they were over 2000 years ago. Empty promises until we decide Christmas is the birth of Jesus in our hearts and not just into the lives of a teenage couple in a time long ago. Empty promises until we decide to make Christmas a year-long, life-long celebration and not one day or a couple of hours out of the whole year. Empty promises until we decide to continue and make happen in this time and place that which God began in a little, dusty, out-of-the-way town called Bethlehem.

Christmas Memories

I remember. I remember when the beginning of the Christmas season was marked by the arrival of the Sears Christmas Catalog, not Labor Day weekend. I remember lying on the floor, wearing out the pages of the toy section in the back of the catalog, wishing, dreaming. Making my list. Knowing that I wouldn't get everything. Hoping I'd get one or two of the toys on my list. Most were outside the parameters of affordability. But, Christmas was the best opportunity to get something I'd not ordinarily have a chance of receiving.

I remember counting the days until Christmas. Each day taking note of the countdown in the lower corner of the first page of the Meridian Star. 25 shopping days until Christmas. Is Christmas still that far off? No, longer. Extra days had to be figured in to the countdown since stores didn't open on Sundays. Waiting. Anticipating. Wishing. Dreaming. Waiting.

I remember when it came time to get a Christmas tree we didn't go to a corner market, grocery store, or home supply center. When it came time to get a Christmas tree we cruised the dusty country roads until we found an acceptable cedar tree growing along the roadside. The tree was cut, carried home, and given a place of honor in our living room. The tree was decked out in strings of multi-colored lights that didn't blink off and on; adorned with metallic red, green, blue, silver, and gold orbs; and then covered (and I mean covered) with shimmering icicles. Mama loved icicles.

I remember. I remember gathering at Grandmama and Granddaddy Taylor's house on Christmas Eve to open presents. I remember waiting, waiting, waiting for Uncle Perry to close his store up the street. No presents would be opened until everyone, including Uncle Perry, was there. It was probably only six o'clock, but it seemed like forever! I remember being bundled up and piled into the car and then chauffeured around town to view the Christmas decorations – creative strategy by our parents to buy time. I remember attending Christmas Eve Communion as a family and then returning home to be tucked warmly in my bed. My bedroom was adjacent to the living room, the site of the imminent clandestine visit, so I went to bed early lest I risk scaring off the midnight rider.

I remember getting up long before daylight on Christmas morning, waking my parents, and pestering them to get up. I remember Mama and Daddy putting us off until the space heater, the only heat source in the front part of the house, could be lighted and the living room be warmed. Waiting. No one could enter the hallowed room until all was ready, and everyone was awake. Waiting, again. I remember walking into the living room on Christmas morning. There was fruit, nuts, and firecrackers. These were standard fare. Then my eyes would wander amidst the wonder to find my bounty. A radio. Or a BB gun. Or a record player – 33 1/3, 45, and 78. Usually one OR the other. Rarely one AND the other. That's what I remember that helped make Christmas special – to get some, not all.

I still remember those smells: a delicate blend of fruit, cedar, and home. I experience those smells from time to time as I push my buggy through the produce department of the grocery store. I have been known to make several trips through the section to inhale again and again and to relive in my memory the Christmas mornings of my childhood. I can still see the Christmas tree standing in the living room of my parents' house, simply but beautifully decorated and undergirded with neatly wrapped presents.

I remember.

Then something happened. My memories of Christmases past changed. Now I remember wondering how in the world everything would get done. Presents to buy. Decorations to hang. Parties to attend. Shopping to do. Food to cook. Visits to make. I remember late night assembly, left over parts. Batteries NOT included? I remember midnight runs to the convenience store. I remember fights in the aisles for Cabbage Patch dolls. Scrambling across town for the last Tickle Me Elmo. Girbaud jeans. The gift wasn't as important as the brand name, the style, the chic. I remember a sense of peace when Christmas, which had dragged on since Labor Day, was finally over.

Something happened. Something changed. I know what it was. I grew up. And Christmas was lost. At least as I like to remember it. No wonderment. Wish lists replaced by to-do lists. No surprises, everything carefully planned and implemented. No anticipation. No Sears and Roebuck Christmas catalogs. Amazon.com. Buy.com. You name it.com. Something happened. Things changed. And I long for the way things used to be.

Call me old-fashioned. Call me old. Call me anything you want. Unrealistic. Idealistic. But I wish for the way things were. Simple. Wonder-filled. Slow. Quiet. The real reason for the season was so much easier to find back then. Not lost behind the glitter. Not crammed in at the last minute. Not in the malls and shopping centers. Back then, the reason for the celebration, the reason for the hoopla, permeated the whole season and everything was a reflection of the birth celebrated.

Gifts, gatherings, food, and festivities. There's nothing wrong with the way we celebrate as long as we remember why we celebrate, who we celebrate. There's nothing wrong with the things we do until the things we do become the reason for the season, an end in themselves. There's nothing wrong with present-day Christmases as long as the gifts, gatherings, food, and festivities become, again, a reflection of the birth celebrated, and the Christ-child is, once more, given center stage. That's what I believe is lost. That's what I hope we can recover. Yet, Christmas will never be as the Christmases I remember until I change and decide to make it so.

Footprints in the Snow

I don't know if I had ever seen it snow sideways. The wind was gusting to nearly 30 miles per hour. The temperature was well below freezing. And it was snowing… hard… sideways. I questioned what I was doing there. We were crazy (probably already a given) to head out into the wilderness in weather like that. It snowed all day long… sideways. We trudge on, determined to reach our destination five miles into the Smoky Mountain backcountry. Snow piled up on the green branches of the evergreen fir trees that, from time to time, sheltered our path and filled the air with their fragrances. The blowing snow clung to the sides of the bare branches of the deciduous trees. We could look off to our left, south, down in the valley and see the town of Cherokee, N.C. The sun was shining. The trees still fully clothed in the splendor of their autumn colors. It looked warm down there. Ahead was cold and blowing snow… Did I mention it was snowing sideways?

The snow continued through the night. We awoke the next morning to brilliant blue skies and a fluffy, blanket of snow; the light of the bright morning sun streaking through the forest and setting off shimmering sparkles on the new-fallen snow. We hiked all the second day under that same blue sky and through what must have been eight inches of snow. My newly purchased gators prevented melted snow from running down into my boots, but hiking was still laborious. I found myself walking in the footsteps of those who hiked ahead of me. It was easier that way. Drier. If that sounds like I was taking advantage of the lead hiker, I was. But that's the role of the lead hiker… to lead the way. The leader makes sure everyone follows the correct path; that the members of the group don't get separated by too great a distance for one to get lost along the way. The leader leaves footprints in the snow or dust or mud, whatever the case may be, that serves to direct others along the way. I took advantage, alright; I took advantage of a good leader who was not going to lead me astray. And the best way to do that was to walk directly in the footprints of those who walked before. Drier, yes. And safer. And more secure. As a follower, I see the stones and roots that hid underneath the snow revealed by the footprints I followed.

As Christians, we have one who has gone before us, leaving footprints into which we may step. These footprints guide us along the way. They show us the safer, more secure way to go. They are footprints that mark the path along which we tread through life. They are the footprints of Jesus. Safer? In many ways, yes. More secure? In many ways, yes. But still dangerous, still challenging, still laborious, still risky. Because these footprints we are called to follow are the footprints of Jesus and they lead to a hill, a hill called Golgotha. The footprints we follow as Christians are the footprints of discipleship and lead to a cross. Are we sure we want to follow?

The Good Ole Days

I've been in sort of midlife crisis lately, I guess, and have purchased CDs of my generation's music. The Allman Brothers Band. Van Morrison. The Beatles' <u>Abby Road</u>. Mac McAnally. John Denver. I've mixed in a few current titles of "my generation's" artists, Santana and Eric Clapton with B. B. King. All those old songs have a way of taking me back to my younger years when life was easier, less pressured, or, at least, when I had more time and energy. The old songs have a way of taking me/us back to the days we consider "the good ole days".

I had the Buddy Miles album years ago but lost it in the Easter Flood of 1979 in Jackson, MS. Eagerly, I inserted CD into the player before I backed out of my parking place. "Carry me back!" The first song I didn't remember. The second song I didn't remember. The third – uh oh. The fourth – nope. No memories connected with these. Purchasing the CD might not have been a good idea. The songs weren't as good as I remembered. I wasn't getting the effect I wanted, and, in a way, needed. Maybe the "good ole days" weren't as good as I remembered, either.

I guess that's the way the past is. We have a tendency to remember the good songs, the good stuff. And as a result, there is this desire to live in the past, to try to keep things the way they were (or the way we remember them), to resist change and, consequently, growth. But life can't be lived in the past, as much as we would like to go back. Sure, the past will always be a part of who we are, but life, regardless of our age, is always in front of us, not behind us. In his closing meditation at this year's annual conference, the Bishop referred to the desire we have to get back to the Bible. The Bible, he said, is not behind us, it is ahead of us. And rather than going back to the Bible, we need to move forward to the Bible. We can't live in the past. We can glance back at the past, the Bishop said, like we keep a check in our rearview mirrors. But life is ahead of us, like the full expanse of our view through the windshield. If we think that the best of life is behind us, we have nothing to live for. If the best of life is still yet to come, then we have everything to live for.

After listening to those first Buddy Miles songs, I scanned ahead to those songs I remembered. Then I popped in Iron Butterfly and scanned forward to "In-A-Gadda-Da-Vida", the album version, with the 10-minute drum solo, and reflected on my younger years. Ah!! Life is good and maybe the past was just as I remember it. And tomorrow can be better.

The
Earth
Speaks

Stormy Weather

The seven-day forecast indicated that today would be a stormy day. A storm would form in Texas and sweep its way through Mississippi bringing heavy rain, strong winds, and possible tornados. We Mississippians know tornados and with the forecast of severe weather in November we remember the tornado that took lives, destroyed homes, and created havoc in our peaceful community just a few years ago. Now the threat of severe weather awakens memories and drives us to cover, one eye on the radar screen and one eye on the sky. Watching. Waiting. Remembering. Storms have a way of doing that to us. When we have been hit once, or twice, or more…

On Monday, the Texas storm started pulling itself together. High winds, torrential rains, and tornados hit the Lone Star State and set their eyes on states to the east. Louisiana was next and then Mississippi. The forecast was for the worst of the weather to move through our area during rush hour. For those whose daily schedule includes fighting heavy traffic and dealing with drivers who don't know how to handle heavy traffic, the storms only complicate their daily routines. The storms mean leaving home and family earlier, allowing for delays. The rain means slick roads and the increased risk of accidents along the way. The threats associated with commutes rise with the wind and rain. Our days our difficult enough without the storms.

Sure enough, as predicted, just as rush hour is beginning, the sky has darkened to the west. My eyes perceive what the local radar indicates. The storms are moving into our area. The winds increase. Lightning streaks from sky to earth. Thunder rumbles above the sounds of the wind. The street lights, fooled to think that it is night, flash on. Then the rain hits. Torrents. Sheets. Windblown. Thoughts of previous storms emerge from the grottoes sheltering our memories. Fear. If damage is going to be done it will be now, at the height of the storm. Precautions are taken. They have been well-rehearsed. Warnings crawl across the bottom to the television screen. Alert ears listen for the sirens. We've been here before. Hoped we wouldn't be here again. But there is never that promise. So, we prepare, we anticipate, we try our best to survive, to rise above the storm.

At the peak of the storm as the winds swirl, as the rain beats down, as we cower in relative safety, it's hard to imagine that there is peace and quiet anywhere. Our whole world is engulfed by the storm, by the darkness. Our whole world is in turmoil, chaos. We would run, but as much as we would like to flee, there is no place to go, no place void of the storms.

In the middle of the tempest it's hard to imagine peace and quiet, but two assurances are ours. One, somewhere up there, somewhere above the storms the sun is shining. Always. Directly above us, if we go high enough, the sky is blue, the sun bright, and the winds calm. Two, as sure as morning follows night, the storm clouds will give way clear skies, the winds will shift, and all will be right in the world again.

As threatening as the storms are, they are temporary. As real as the storms are, they are momentary. As always, as we flee, cower, or fight, our hope is in knowing that this, too, shall pass. The healing north winds will come. Our spirits lifted. The sun will shine. Our lives brightened and warmed. But that is tomorrow's forecast. For today, we have to endure the storms. Stay tuned. Stay alert. Stay strong. Stay cautious. Stay hopeful. Hope-full for the sun is always shining. The weather will change. The winds will calm. The rain will cease. The skies will clear. Tomorrow will come.

Roly Polies

They looked like stars in the dark night sky. Twinkling. Glittering. Disappearing as if some fast-moving, silent cloud was drifting by. I first thought they were lightning bugs. Those fascinating insects we chased around the yard as kids. Grabbing and grasping with clinched fists, careful not to squish them in our palms, so we could capture their light in a Mason jar or as a ring around our finger. But as I observed in the darkness of the North Carolina mountains, I noticed that these sparkling lights never rose above the ground. Curious, I twisted the end of my Mini-Maglite and set off on a fact-finding expedition. To seek out the source of the luminous green lights in the grass.

I expected them to be spider eyes. I had discovered spider eyes on a backpacking trip on the Black Creek several years ago with a couple of friends. A head lamp directed into the eyes of spiders seeking their evening meal will glow with an eerie light as it is reflected or refracted in the spiders' eyes. The mystery lights on the ground in Lost Mine Campground could not be spider eyes since whatever the source, it was evidently producing its own light. Bioluminescence, for the inquisitive. So, with flashlight in hand and my buddies consuming cashews and other treats back at the camper, I set out to resolve the great nightlight mystery.

As a light flickered in the night, I would mark the spot with the beam of my light and then move silently toward the source of the light, only to have the light dim and then extinguished as if snuffed out. After several attempts, I finally was able to move to the source of the light in time. There I found a small creature roaming through the grass like a wild animal through the woods.

The creature appeared to be a roly poly, a small terrestrial crustacean capable of rolling itself into a ball. Another of our "play pretties" when we were young. Entertainment was cheap when I was growing up. Give me a few roly polies to roll around in my palm or to tickle my hand as they ran for safety. Lightning bugs. Fishing for doodle bugs with a piece of pine straw. But I had never heard of a light-producing roly poly. I don't even remember one being discussed in my graduate biology classes at Mississippi College. Although I spent many hours wading in the Chunky Creek cataloging Mayflies and other aquatic insects, reptiles, amphibians, and fishes.

After tracking down several more of these baffling and peculiar organisms, I was sure that I had found the source of the mystifying glow in the night. Upon my return home I sought my entomology textbooks to see if I could identify the creature. I was surprised to find several light-producing organisms among the insects and crustaceans. However, I could not reach any conclusive identification of the source of the light. Somewhere I'm sure somebody knows.

I am forever amazed at the creativity of our creating God. How often do we miss the Creator because we take God's creation for granted, unable to see the diversity of life formed from the imagination of God; failing to see the wonder of God's ingenious mind and artistic hands; demanding the more and more spectacular and sensational in order to believe in miracles? How often do we miss the Creator because we misunderstand the meaning of dominion, and tiller, and stewardship; believing God's gifts are free for us to use and abuse as we see fit; inconsiderate of future generations? How often do we miss the Creator because we are too busy and too preoccupied with business and activity to see and experience the goodness of creation and our relationship to the earth? How often do we miss the Creator and the wonders of life?

Let's open our eyes to the splendor. Breathe deep of the fragrances. Listen to the voices. Feel the textures. Savor the flavors. Celebrate life and our oneness with all the creatures of the world. And be still and know God, the Creator.

In the Garden

Each summer over most of the years of my life there have been at least tomatoes planted. Those plants would provide fresh, home-grown tomatoes for tomato sandwiches on white bread with real mayonnaise. Those plants would provide tomatoes to enhance a meal of fresh veggies from back home, generous gifts from our parents and grandparents.

As far back as I can remember there was always a large garden behind Percy and Louisa's house next door to ours. Percy and Louisa were my Granddaddy and Grandmama Taylor, Daddy's parents and we shared garden space – Daddy's rows of vegetables and their rows. Tended, kept, fertilized and watered. Picked, shelled, cooked, served and preserved.

My first garden was a part of that larger family garden. Since it was "my" garden, it was my responsibility to prepare, plant, tend, keep, and pick. I've always loved gardening, there is just something special about preparing the soil, planting the seeds, caring for the young, tender plants, watching nature at its best – preserving its own kind, reproducing, fruiting. One generation giving birth to the next generation through procreation and proliferation. The new generation giving birth to the next. The next generation... The plant's sole responsibility is to flower and fruit, to form the seeds that give rise to future generations and ensure the continuation of the species. Of course, it is those fruits, those seeds that are the vegetables that we eat to nurture and sustain us, to provide the energy we need, to supply the nutrients our bodies crave. Not to mention, they are those veggies that we love to eat because they taste soooooo good.

I guess because I shared garden space with Daddy and Granddaddy, gardening is also a way that I remain connected. Connected to family and the generations of Taylors, Kemps, Eaves, and Masseys that gardened before me. Connected to all those generations before me who

122

lived close to the earth and depended on it to provide the necessities of life. Gardening is a way that I remember and remain connected especially to my own parents for whom gardening was a way of life and a way of living. It was as much a part of their lives as their breath, as getting up and going to work on Monday mornings, as washing, ironing, cooking, and cleaning. On hot summer mornings while the dew was wet on the vines, I could always find Daddy out in the garden, hidden among the dense vines and tall stalks. Years later on weekend visits Daddy and I would walk the rows of his garden, not just to check out the plants and observe their growth, but to allow our lives to continue to grow together and intertwine like the vines in the garden.

In June on the day before Father's Day, I walked around and through my garden in the back yard of our home in Madison. Father's Day was not on my mind, but Daddy was. As I examined my plantings, I remembered him standing among the bean poles and tomato plants. As I walked along the rows, I remembered our walks. As I took the runaway vines of the green beans and lima beans and wrapped them around the twine and wire supports, I talked with Daddy and regretted not "sticking" the beans as he had.

In the garden we were so close, on that Saturday as in the past. That closeness was found not just in the memories but in the vines of our lives that remain intertwined one with the other. The connectedness of our lives is found literally in the green bean vines in my garden that have grown profusely from seeds, but not just any store-bought seeds. They're Daddy's seeds. As I walked down that row of green bean vines, I was about as close to Daddy as I could physically get. Plants from Daddy's seeds. Found in the freezing unit of an old refrigerator at Mama and Daddy's house. Saved year after year to give birth to a new generation. Now passed to me and planted in my garden to provide for me and my family in the way that they provided for Daddy and his family, and Granddaddy and his family. Seeds sown in faith and abundance to carry on that which had been passed on, from one generation to the next, from one family to the next, from one man's life to the next. Sowing those seeds that ensure the continuation of life and exemplify the connectedness of all generations, of all people.

Back to the Garden

The squash and zucchini have come and gone, falling victim to the heat and humidity. But they were good while they lasted. Stewed with onions. Breaded and fried. Marinated and grilled. The cucumbers are gone. At least one vine falling victim to the string of the weedeater. We did get some pickles, though. The okra plants are tall and still producing at the rate of a harvest every other day or so. The tomato plants have grown out over their wire stands and continue to produce fruit even though they were threatened by a recent stinkbug infestation. Nothing that a little Sevin wouldn't stop. So, the tomato sandwiches have returned to the lunch and dinner menu. Still, wheat bread and light Helman's mayo. Weight Watchers, you know. For some reason our pepper plants, banana and green, struggle in our garden, but the few remaining plants are providing a few fruits to enhance recipes and veggies.

The green beans, the ones planted from my Daddy's seeds, those seeds found in one of their three refrigerators back in the winter, and the butter (lima) beans are another matter. With great care I prepared the soil, spread grass cloth to control the weeds, placed the seeds in shallow holes, watered and fed. The seeds sprouted, and the vines grew. I strung wire and string between posts on which the vines have thrived. Early in the summer we picked fruits from both, green beans and butter beans. Delicious. Throw a few pods of okra in with the butter beans and boil them together, dice in a little pepper, slice a fresh tomato, add a serving of green beans – it just doesn't get any better. Who needs meat with a meal of fresh veggies from the garden?

Something happened. The vines continued to grow, but they have produced little if any fruit. Even today the vines are green, lush, beautiful, covering everything in sight. Intertwining around themselves, each other, the adjacent tomato plants. Covering the wire, string, and posts. Flourishing. Thriving. Growing. But few if any blooms. Little if any fruits. I'm at a loss. There has been ample rainfall to quench the thirst of the growing plants. I have kept the weeds at bay. I have fed to stimulate development and maturity. But no fruit. No servings of fresh veggies on the dinner table. No green beans to snap, cook, eat. Plenty of okra, but no butter beans in which to boil the pods.

What to do? One would think that with vines so thick and healthy that there would be plenty of fruit. Enough for the dinner table. Enough to share. But the vines are just not producing fruit. I guess the only thing I can do is pull up the vines and toss them in the trash. I don't want vines, no matter how beautiful they look, no matter how healthy they appear. I didn't plant the seeds to produce vines. I planted the seeds for vines that would produce veggies. What good are vines if they don't produce fruit? They're just occupying space. Space that can be used to plant seeds that perhaps will produce the fruits that will satisfy our cravings, our hungers, our needs. Perhaps I need to get out in the garden soon, take down the wire and string, pull up the plants, and discard them in the compost pile. Did I mention that the vines are beautiful? But they're producing no fruit and as such are really of no use to anyone.

Jesus said, "I am the vine, you are the branches. Those who abide in me and I in them bear much fruit... Whoever does not abide in me is thrown away like a branch and withers; such branches are gathered, thrown into the fire, and burned." (John 15:5ff)

One thing, Jesus wasn't talking about green beans and butter beans.

Tropical Storm Matthew

I guess some people thought I was crazy. On my bicycle in the wind, rain, and high surf. Out in the midst of the storm when I could have been safely tucked in the security of the house, big-screen TV, college football, golf... nap. Instead, I hopped on my bike and peddled down to the beachfront and stood with my face to the wind. It was an awesome experience feeling the power of the wind, rain, and spray of the surf in my face. Crazy? Maybe.

I have, for many years, watched with fascination as storms approached coastal areas of the southeast. I have watched, that is, from the safe distances to the north. When we moved to the coast we knew the threat of hurricanes, a knowledge gained only by watching from a distance. With each storm report I watched as people moved from the safety and security of homes and shelters to stand in the wind and the rain, to feel the power of the storm. I often questioned their sanity, too.

When Ivan approached the coast in September, the threat was more than I wanted to face, more than I wanted to experience first-hand. I know some chose to stay and ride it out. But, not me. Not my first storm. I figured the best defense is a good offense. So, we protected property as best as we could and headed for the safe havens to the north and waited it out. Watching on television those people out in the midst of the storm their hair peeled back by the wind, bracing themselves against the force, feeling the power, enduring the threat.

Sometimes, I have learned, the storms can be avoided, escaped, and safety and security can be found in safe havens away from the force of the storm. Sometimes there is no escape, nowhere to run, nowhere to hide. Sometimes the only choice we have, or a valid choice we make, is to ride out the storm. But we do so only with a different strategy, another defensive tactic to face the threat, to endure, to survive.

As the winds and rain of Matthew lashed the shore line I observed the seagulls, the pelicans, and other birds who rode out the storm. I watched with particular interest the seagulls that tend to huddle together or line the piers or feed along the beach in flocks. At the height of the storm, the seagulls that never escaped the wrath of the storm faced the storm together in their flocks. Safety and security, survival, was possible as they persevered together. However, the seagulls had another amazing, precautionary strategy that I observed – they turned their faces to the wind. They faced the storm head on. They didn't turn their backs, or their sides, to the force of the wind and rain. Stability in the midst of the forces that buffeted the coast and threatened their lives was found in confronting the storm straight on. Their best defense, their best offense, was to deal with the force, the threat, face to face.

By late Sunday afternoon, though the remnants of Matthew continued, I could tell the storm was over. The clouds broke, the sun shone through. Behind those clouds, wind, and rain the sun had never stopped shining. Hidden from view, but still shining. Folks ventured out onto the beachfront for the first time. No longer hunkered down. Having survived, the birds sailed. A trawler made its way into the Gulf. The storm had passed. Life was returning to normal.

Sometimes we are fortunate to be able to escape the storms, by choice or by luck. We find safe havens away from the wind and the rain. Many times, most of the time, we don't have that opportunity and the only choice we have is to ride out the storm. We survive when we face the storms together in community. We survive when we turn our faces to the wind and meet the challenges head on.

The Trout Lily

Blooming on the moist hillsides before the trees put on their leaves in the mountains of North Carolina there is a wildflower that produces a single elegant yellow flower on the end of a long stalk that extends upward from a base of two elongated leaves. The wildflower is called a trout lily, so named because of the mottled appearance of the leaves that resembles the brook trout. The trout lily is a delight to the eyes and a pleasure to photograph, particularly if the fiddlehead of a nearby fern fits into the frame.

Other than the beauty of the flower, an interesting characteristic of this plant, according to my references, is its slow growth and low reproduction. It may take seven years or more for the plant to flower. Seven or more years!! An acorn can grow into a sizable tree in that period of time. A child can go from the first grade to a teenager in seven years. And an average driver will go through 2 or more cars. The trout lily probably would not be the flower of choice for those of us who have become accustomed to instant gratification.

If the trout lily causes you to rethink the pace and the haste of our lives, consider the white trillium that transforms the brown forest floor of winter into a profusion of white in the spring. Trillium seeds are well adapted for being carried away by insects. They have an ant-snack, a chemical attractant, which drives ants into a feeding frenzy. Ants take the seeds to their nests, eat the "ant-snack," and then discard the seeds in their tunnels where they germinate in large numbers. But, still, white trilliums need to grow for 15 years before they flower. Fifteen years!! Talk about delayed gratification! From the time the seed germinates, and the first flower appears, my child leaves the playpen and gets behind the steering wheel.

Now I know I'm spoiled, as we all are. I practice delayed gratification. Since the crust is my least favorite part, I eat the crust of the pie first and save the inner tasty wedge for last. In this day and time, we are pushed more toward instant gratification. In this digital age, we've forgotten that television sets used to have to "warm up" before the picture appeared. Hungry? Throw an instant meal into the microwave and zap it for a few seconds. Instant potatoes. Instant coffee. Want your coffee perked? Drip coffeemakers. Changing channels? Preset push-button controls. Why wait when you can have it now?

We tend to live our lives in such a rush; we can pass right by the flower that has been fifteen years in the making. We can miss the miracles that materialize right before our eyes. We can fail to grasp the mysteries that appear in our midst. And though we have been called by God to be the sowers of the seeds of God's love and grace, rather than sowing with reckless abandon we tend to hold the seeds in tightly-clinched fists, unable to risk the wait for the fruits that will appear, not in our time, but in God's.

Those Darling Starlings

The starlings have arrived. In all their numbers. In all their force. They have arrived. When they arrive the other birds scatter. Chickadees, titmice, wrens, sparrows, and goldfinches are no match for the greed and gluttony of the starlings. Not even the redbirds in their number can match that of the starlings. I despise the starlings. Not because they're ugly. Actually, they are beautiful. Their black feathers are iridescent in the winter sun. Subtle colors of purple and shades of green reflect as the sun's rays are bent through the fine fibers of the feathers. I despise the starlings. Not because of their size. I despise them because of the way they throw their weight around. Not because of their numbers. But, because of the way they use their numbers to intimidate the others and take over the feeders. I despise the starlings. I love the underdogs, the vulnerable. I love the small, the cute. I ache for those who are forced to flee for their lives and seek security in the branches and the bushes out on the fringes of my backyard.

In my spite for the starlings I have emerged from my own refuge onto the cold concrete patio and created a noisy disturbance to frighten the starlings away. However, they're not dumb. They take flight to the nearest tree top and there wait for me to go back inside. Sometimes I try different measures to harass the pests. I hurl rocks at the birds on their perch. Like I said, they're not dumb. They know my range and fly just beyond to the next tree tops and there wait me out for they know I'll disappear back into the safe haven of my den. After a while they'll return, take over, pig out.

Desperate situations require desperate measures. So, sometimes I hire a hit man. The starlings are the only bird I have given Ben permission to shoot with his BB gun. (Yes, I'm ashamed. But, they say confession is good for the soul.) I'll avoid the details of his cunning assassination plots. Yet, however cunning or shrewd or well-planned his strategy, the starlings still come, in just as many numbers, with their same instincts and attitudes. Oh, there are other tactics to rid my yard of the unwanted and undesirables. But, the city of Madison has ordinances and laws against the use of such firepower.

It would be easy for me to simply withdraw to the comfort of my couch where harmony reigns and the fire is warm. It would be simple for me to ignore the conflict outside my windows. It would be easy for me to turn power over to the starlings. Or maybe there is another way, another tactic, another strategy. It is easy to forget that the starlings are just doing what comes naturally. Even the starlings get hungry. Even the starlings need care. Even the starlings need nourishment and feeding. And when I placed my feeders in my backyard, I invited them to feed, whether I want to admit it or not. Though the starlings are greedy, selfish, insensitive, overpowering – they are God's creatures, too. Just like the cute ones and the small ones. Ultimately, there is no distinction. The only distinctions are those I make out of my prejudices and my own preferences. Nor can I change them. I can't make them be something they're not, something they can't be.

I have a choice. I can continue to pester the starlings in the hopes of running them off. Experience has proven that won't happen. Or...I can throw rocks to frighten them into going to a feeder in someone else's backyard. Experience has proven that won't happen either. Or...I can bring out more firepower and blast them into oblivion. That strategy, in addition to being dangerous, is unethical not to mention unlawful. As creatures of the Creator there must be another way.

I have learned that they make birdfeeders just for little birds. Feeders for the small, the cute, the loveable, the vulnerable. With a little added expense, I can add a few of those feeders and the chickadees, wrens, titmice, redbirds, and other defenseless birds can be fed without fear and without intimidation. Lo and behold with a little effort, a little understanding, and a little compassion on my part the starlings and the chickadees can feast together. The powerful and powerless. The strong and the weak. The indomitable and the vulnerable. All God's creatures get fed. All get what they seek. All get what they need. Everyone has a place at the table.

Bluets

I always look for them this time of year. In fact, I usually write about them. Especially when I see the first ones of the spring. They're magical to me, special. They remind me of my college days. ECCC. George Mason. Botany class. In the spring we had to have a wild-flower collection. Wild flowers. Not domesticated. Not homegrown. Not cultivated. Wild flowers. Of course, in the spring there is no shortage of wildflowers, particularly for one who will only open his/her eyes to the beauty surrounding us. Most of us have another name we use. Weeds. But if one looks closely enough the "weeds" possess dainty, pastel-colored flowers which sometimes grow in such numbers that they turn the whole landscape into a painting even the most talented artist could never capture. Spring beauties. Henbit. Johnny Jump Ups. Wild buttercups. As many as the stars in the sky.

Last Friday I saw one of my favorites. I had gotten away for a couple of days to papaw's farm in Newton County. Drive the tractor. Fish. Ride the four-wheeler. You know, get away. Let the fog clear, so to speak. Re-focus. Re-center. Recreate. I was tugging a small trailer across the old garden site when something caught my eye. Could it be? This early in the year? I pushed the trailer back a few steps and looked again. There it was. A single, solitary blossom. Just a speck of sky blue in an ocean of brown. A bluet. *Houstonia patens.* I love the bluets. The epitome of dainty. The essence of pastel.

All winter long they have been waiting. Waiting for the first warm days of late winter, early spring. I don't know if they are annuals or perennials. I don't really care. I just see them when they arrive in spring and grace the roadsides, trail sides, and pathways with their presence. A rite of springtime. Spring, whether the calendar substantiates it or not, spring has arrived. The landscape is about to undergo a dramatic, colorful transformation. It's a sign. No, more than a sign. It's an epiphany. A revelation. New life. The old has gone. The new has come. Death will not have the final word. Winter will pass, and spring will come. An extreme makeover. Transformation. Resurrection.

Ever since last spring, lying dormant beneath the leaves, under the brown grass, new life has waited for the right time. Surviving the droughts of summer. Enduring the frosts of fall. Clinging to hope under the snow and ice of winter. Waiting for the right time. For its time.

130

Hope. Promise. Assurance. Potential. Yes, potential. Lying just below the surface. Unseen. Unknown. Potential. And just at the right time, when God's time and our time miraculously intersect. Potential no more.

There is something special down deep within each of us as well. Something good. Something worthy. It's been there since the beginning. Yet, hidden and in some instances suppressed. Down within each of us behind the masks, behind the façade. Suppressed by ego, concealed by self-interests, covered up by human tendencies and sin. There lies deep within each of us, within every person, a seed. Potential, just waiting to be discovered, just waiting to be recovered and fulfilled. A seed waiting to be nourished and cultivated. A seed that has potential for good beyond human comprehension. Just waiting. It has been there from the beginning and will never be completely destroyed or lost, for God will not allow it. So, it waits. For you, for me. Deep with each of us is a seed of great potential. *Imago Dei.* The very Image of God. What a different world this would be if we nurtured within ourselves and saw within others the image of God!

Hummers

In the backyard under the elm tree I've erected a birdfeeder post that offers four feeders to entice birds from the surrounding woodlands into view from the patio. One feeder offers thistle seeds in the hopes of luring goldfinches in their brilliant yellow summer plumage. A bright red feeder holds a rich sugar-water mixture to nourish and energize the hummingbirds. Two feeders are filled with a mixture of seeds, nuts, and fruits to tantalize any songbirds hiding in the thicket.

So far only the hummers have come. Most other birds have a smorgasbord of food provided by nature itself as we near the fall harvest. Seeds, nuts, fruits hanging within easy reach of their hiding places, not having to venture into the open to feed at the table I've spread. But, they will come. Later, their natural offerings will be depleted, and my table will be set. All will be welcome.

Meanwhile, the hummers have come. First, one. Then, a second. Now, four or five. They move in such haphazard and rapid motion among the trees it's hard for me to keep count. They are a sight to behold. Zipping here and there. One after another like a dogfight between two high tech fighter jets. Zooming undeterred by the obstacles that would act as a dart board should one fail to negotiate a turn. Speeding through trunks, limbs, and leaves without the aid of radar. Swarming the feeder like bees around a beehive. One can easy laugh at their antics, their apparent playfulness, one with another. Until one realizes that it is not play. What appears to be fun-filled clowning around is really behavior borne out of jealousy, fear, and insecurity. Territorialism.

Out of the five hummingbirds who visit my feeder none really get a chance to eat. Acting out of instinct, one bird assumes the dominant role and takes control of the feeder. The dominant hummer continually bars any of the other hungry birds from feasting at my table. What appears to be a game of chase among the flowers and trees is really an attack. It really is more of a dogfight than we realize. The intimidator refuses to allow any other hummer to perch and sip the rich nectar. And... so intent is the intimidator to exclude all others, that neither does it have a chance to feast. All of the dominate bird's energy and attention is devoted to keeping the "underlings" away from the table. So frightened and controlling is that one bird that none get to eat at the table. A table with a place for all.

To observe such conduct is disheartening. The tiny birds are so cute, seemingly so helpless, so vulnerable. One would not imagine that a creature of God's creating would behave in a way that would serve to dominate, control, and victimize another. However, this type of behavior is not unusual in nature. In fact, dominating behavior is quite common among the various species of the animal kingdom.

Back in my previous life as a science teacher, I filled my classroom with aquaria, cages, and displays. Crawfish, native fish, snakes, insects, a guinea pig, and two black gerbils which almost overnight became six or eight. I "stocked" one aquarium with four bream I had collected from a small pond. Almost immediately one fish took control and "herded" the other three into a corner. That one dominant fish consumed all the food and prevented the others from venturing out into the open water of the aquarium. To alleviate the situation, I decided to remove the dominant fish and place it in another aquarium. Lo and behold, as soon as I removed that fish another fish took over the dominant role and intimidation – consumed all the food and kept other two remaining fish confined in the corner.

Homo sapiens (humans) as a species within the animal kingdom are also prone to exhibit similar behaviors related to territorialism. We, too, have our territories to defend even though the territory is really not ours to own. We, too, have our tendencies to intimidate others, especially those we perceive to be inferior or subordinate. We, too, exert an awful amount of energy and devote an awful lot of our attention to fending off "threats" to our security. We, too, deny access to a table set for all with plenty for all.

Though we are scientifically "animals" we rest at the pinnacle of creation, gifted with a conscious, reason, and a soul. We have been given a "heart" that rests in the bosom of God. "Then God said, 'Let us make humankind in our image, according to our likeness...'" (Genesis 1:26) We have been created in the image of God. In turn, we will hopefully exhibit behaviors above that of the other animals in God's creation.

Berries and Birds

I spot them through the blinds of our back door and windows. There was another one this morning – another bird in my blueberries. Another bird attracted by those luscious fruits and through sheer determination has found or made a way to get through the protective (?) netting. How do those guys do it?!?! I've stitched up holes with garbage bag ties, weighted down the edges with bricks and boards, and stapled the net to poles. But, no matter how hard I try, no matter what I do, the birds find a way in. The bird finds a way in but can't find a way out. So, here I go, traipsing out in the backyard through the wet grass in my bare feet to get the bird out before he eats up my berries.

The best way I've found to get them out is to raise up the net on one end and then move around the bushes to chase the bird to that end. The only problem is birds tend to fly on a level or upward course, not down toward the ground. Thus, I must walk around and around as the bird flies back and forth under the net. I hope the neighbors don't watch. A video would probably win the grand prize. Finally (hopefully), the bird will fly into the net at the open end, fall to the ground, discover the ground-level escape hatch, and takeoff to freedom.

On one occasion, the bird would not cooperate. Around and around I went. Back and forth the bird flew, never falling to the ground. Eventually, I had to climb inside the netting with the bird, trap the bird, and grasp him in my hands (cringing at the thought of being pecked by the angry bird's beak – Mockingbirds have that reputation, you know). Out of exhaustion or confusion or compassion or gratitude, I don't know which, the bird opted not to peck. I took him to the opening and set him free.

Like Mockingbirds we are drawn to, tempted and ensnared by various "delicious fruits" of our world and culture. The resulting mess we may call the "human predicament" or the "human condition" is one from which we cannot save ourselves. Sometimes we will go to the ends of the earth in an effort to reach the "fruits" but try as we might, we can't get out, we cannot save ourselves. The only thing, the only way, we can be saved is through the grace of God. God's grace didn't get us into the fix we're in, our free will takes care of that for us. It is God's grace that sets us free. "For God so loved the world...," John 3:16 says. We are saved by God's never-ending desire to save. We are saved because God was willing to come to us as one of us in the person of Jesus Christ, reach down into the entanglement of our lives, lift us out of the muck and mire, and set us free. In the person of Jesus Christ God did for us what we cannot do for ourselves.

The difference between what I did for the birds and what God did for us is – what I did I did for the sake of the fruit; what God did he did for me... and you.

The Omen

Every now and then we are given the opportunity to witness an event that delights our senses and overwhelms our senses. If we are lucky, fortunate, or, better yet, blessed we become a part of the experience and we are transformed. Suddenly, life is new, our vision is clearer, and our understanding is deepened.

In his book, The Tracker, Tom Brown calls such an event an omen. Normally, we think an omen is a harbinger of doom and gloom. Brown says that "an omen is an experience that interprets all events that follow it and reinterprets everything that went before."[iii] "Once someone has experienced an omen that person will never be the same," says Brown.[iv] As people inclined toward the typical definition of omen, we can perhaps use the more familiar Biblical term, revelation. Scripturally, we are talking about Moses on Mt. Sinai, Noah and the rainbow, Jesus on the Mount of Transfiguration, the Resurrection of Christ. Certainly, John on Patmos.

Of course, an omen doesn't have to be an event of Biblical proportions. I remember visiting George and Frances Spring one afternoon on their front porch where they were watching the hummingbirds swarm the feeder like bees. One of the birds, in its rambunctious attempt to get to the feeder, injected its beak into the screen of the porch. Unable to escape its snare, the tiny bird was rescued by Miss Frances. When I arrived to visit I found Miss Frances cradling the wounded hummer in her cupped hands resting in her lap. An illustration of providential care.

A favorite hymn sung as the setting sun filters through the stained-glass windows. A rainbow that ends in the freshly-baled hay field. The millions of "diamonds" formed on the shoulders of tiny ripples in the winter sun. The first whimper of a new-born baby. A familiar fragrance. A beloved scripture read for the bazillionth time, but this time... Through these seemingly small events something else is at work, the Spirit of God, to bring a new meaning and a more profound understanding to the times of our life.

While visiting friends in Pascagoula a couple of years ago Susan walked out to get something from our truck. On her way she found a baby squirrel, perhaps four months old, lying injured on the Walker's concrete driveway. To many, the helpless creature was nothing special. To many, it is one of God's precious creatures. Acknowledging that there is no morality in nature and that nature has its established cycles of life, some would have left the creature to die, or at least to come what may. Some, like Alice, Susan, and me, would intervene. And, we did. The squirrel was too young to fend for itself. Too injured to escape a raptor's grasp. Too vulnerable. Too needy. Too helpless.

Fortunately, Alice's husband, Russ, is a vet. While I kept the squirrel's attention, Alice crept up from behind and enveloped it in the soft nap of a towel. Quickly, Alice was off to Russ' clinic. If it had to die, at least it would die without further suffering. If its injuries could be treated, Russ would do that. The diagnosis, however, was good. No broken bones. The prognosis bright. Stunned, but okay. The best care

135

would come, not from well-intended humans, not from a trained veterinarian, but from the squirrel's mother. The vet's prescription was written to us, not the squirrel.

Alice is small in stature and not even a ladder lifted her high enough into the Live Oak tree. After stabilizing the ladder, I climbed to the top rung with the lowest fork in the tree within reach. Alice carefully handed me the warm bundle and I cradled it in my cupped hands. With as much caution as possible I placed the baby squirrel in the embrace of the sturdy oak.

Unbeknownst to us, our entire adventure had been under the watchful eye of the baby's mother high above in the Live Oak tree. Even as I placed the tiny squirrel securely in the tree, its mother scurried through the limbs and leaves toward her baby. Alice alerted me to the mother squirrel's movements. While I was still on the top of the ladder, she reached her injured baby. She nuzzled the infant and obviously sensed the smell of human hands. Without further hesitation, she grasped her baby in her mouth and scurried back to her nest high in the arms of the Live Oak tree.

In all my years in the outdoors, I'd never witnessed such love and care in the natural world. I was amazed. Nature had given me a parable of the providential care of God and a new perspective on life.

The Sentinel Oak

The torso-sized lower limbs of the majestic oak span a good hundred feet. They extend like out-stretched arms to grasp rays of sunlight to provide food and energy for the massive tree. To provide shelter and protection for wanderers caught in a summer downpour. To serve as the rungs on a ladder for a child to climb high to gaze out, around, and down. Noooo! Don't look down! Like the magnolia tree we climbed as children in my grandparent's backyard, to a child those first limbs would seem a mile high. A youngster would wait for years for the time they could be gripped on a decent vertical leap. From there the limbs would simply be the steps of a winding staircase leading to the last branches large enough for support and provide a view out into the world of the child's imagination. The crow's nest on the pirate ship's tallest mast. The tower of the castle. Perhaps a watch tower to scour the horizon for the approaching enemy. As a child if I had had this monster tree in my backyard there's no doubt that mismatched scraps of lumber would have scaled the trunk to provide access to the secret tree house hidden in the limbs and leaves above. A place of solitude, respite, feelings of security. Today having access to nails, boards, and the tree, I, over 60 years of age, still haven't ruled out the tree house.

The oak tree is a white oak. Its girth four feet from the ground is twelve feet. Using a formula developed by someone smarter than myself I calculate the tree to be 229 years old. The white oak, as majestic as it is massive began its growth from a single acorn somewhere around the year 1783. A single acorn germinating in the new age of freedom following the Revolutionary War sent roots deep into the red earth of eastern Newton County to provide nourishment for growth and strength to withstand hurricane-force winds and the bite of the axe. Limbs like arms raised in praise to its Creator. The limbs and leaves extending outward and upward, grasping the light, "breathing" the air.

Two hundred and twenty-nine years ago. 1783. It's hard to believe the oak was not chopped or sawed in its earlier years to provide wood to stoke a fireplace on cold winter nights. 229 years. In the Tallashua Creek nearby a lot of water has flowed under the bridge in that length of time. Since the acorn germinated in the red clay, the land on which the grand oak stands has been owned by nine families. Timber has been cut. The land cultivated. Cattle have grazed. The springs have flowed with the water for life. Adventurers, homesteaders, and travelers crossed the land on the old Jackson (or as we Newton Countians prefer, Decatur) - Meridian Road. In 1862 Pvt. John Wesley Cross serving in Company D, 3rd Regiment of the Mississippi Infantry of the Confederate States Army died of the measles while trying to get home to his wife and two sons in Duffee. It was in the spring and the creeks were high. Pvt. Cross is buried in a family cemetery back in the woods with a dozen, or so, others known only to God. In 1864 General William Tecumseh Sherman moving 20,000 troops from Vicksburg entered Newton County near the community now known as Conehatta. After spending the night in or near Decatur and burning virtually every building in town, he, too, traversed the land via the Decatur – Meridian Road. War and peace. Drought and flood. Prosperity and poverty. Life and death. The 229-year-old oak has seen it all. Withstood it all.

In 2018 the tree is still clinging to life on the hillside behind the barn of an old home place. While not the centerpiece of the old homestead the white oak is certainly the sentinel. Hidden from view by the encroaching new generation of forest. Forgotten, too, perhaps as the inhabitants of this country place have also given way to subsequent generations of hard working families. The land and home place, for the most part, are quiet now. The centerpiece, the wood-frame, enclosed dog-trot home struggles to survive as old houses do when their families are gone. The life-giving spirit of family dissipates. The house gives up. But the sentinel, the 229-year-old white oak, still lives to stand guard over the vacant land, to endure the changes that come with the passage of time, to resist the destructive forces of nature, and to tell its story to all who will pause beneath its out-stretched limbs. A story that speaks of the strength, stability, and resilience of roots deeply grounded in the firm foundation of faith. A story that speaks of the life possible as our arms stretch heavenward and empty hands open to receive the gift of love. A story that speaks of joy unimaginable as we raise our faces toward the Son and breathe deep the Spirit of grace. The sentinel stands, watches, waits. Let us stop and listen. For we still have much to learn.

In Closing

When the Well Runs Dry

Well, here I am again. In my usual Tuesday morning place. In my desk chair with my laptop computer. The dim glow of the lamp illuminating my study. Chelsea, our Corgi, is cozily stretched out on the carpet at my feet. Here I am again, writing my newsletter article. From this spot I've reflected on the birds outside at my feeders. I've reflected on my garden and whitewater paddling. I've reflected on the lives and deaths of my parents. Reflected on weeds and seeds, family and friends, God and life. Thinking theologically, I reflect on common, everyday life and how we find, feel, see, experience, learn about God. Sometimes those ideas and meditations come easily. Sometimes they don't. Today is one of those times when the ideas and meditations haven't come easily. I've looked out the backdoor. At the garden and the yard. At the cats. At Chelsea. At the Gulf of Mexico as the waves lazily lap at the seawall. Nothing. Not that the messages aren't there. Today for some reason I can't hear them speak. It's difficult to hear when the well runs dry.

Usually when the ideas and meditations just won't come, I pull a folder from my filing cabinet, the folder labeled "Good Stuff" and copy something that might be meaningful or entertaining. But, I'm at home, on the couch. My folder is at the church. Which seems to be miles away. A long way away when the well runs dry.

Back in my previous life, back before seminary, back when I was a high school physics teacher, I taught my students wave theory. Longitudinal and compression. Sound waves, if I remember correctly, are compression waves. When a rock is thrown into a pond longitudinal waves are formed. Waves that move out from the point of impact in a series of crests and troughs. Amplitude is the height of a wave. Wavelength is the, you guessed it, the length of the wave. Frequency is the number of waves that pass a given point within a specific period of time. Every longitudinal wave consists of a crest and a trough. (You never know what you may learn when you read these articles, huh?)

Sounds like life, doesn't it? Crests and troughs. Mountains and valleys. Highs and lows. Times when the water moves fresh and cold and times when the well runs dry. Times when the Spirit moves as freely as the morning north wind after the violence of the evening storms. Times when the Spirit seems as still as the doldrums of a Mississippi August afternoon. Oh, the Spirit is always there, always fresh, always moving.

So, the fault is not with the Spirit. There's no doubt in our minds about that... when we're on top, on the crests, on spiritual highs. But down in the valleys, in the troughs, when the well runs dry... doubt, forsakenness, and loneliness prevail.

We love the highs. We love the mountaintops. We love the crests. Yet, we can't avoid the valleys. We can't avoid the lows, the troughs. "Let us stay here on the mountaintop," says Peter. "We have to go back down into the valley," says Jesus. Both are times of trial. Do we remember God when we're up on the mountaintop and everything is going our way? Can we trust God, and let God be God, when we're in the valleys and nothing is going our way? Life is both. Crests and troughs. Highs and lows. Mountains and valleys. And one is usually followed by the other. The mountains prepare us for the valleys and the valleys, if we trust and are patient enough, will soon pass and we'll be on top again.

Psalm 22 expresses the emotions of the valley: forsakenness, abandonment, loneliness, doubt. Psalm 22 expresses those emotions so well that Jesus quoted the psalm as he hung on the cross. Psalm 22 echoes our emotions when we pass through the valleys of our lives. As I read Psalm 22 I am aware of the juxtaposition of that psalm and the next, The Twenty-Third Psalm. The forsakenness of Psalm 22 followed immediately by the faith of the Twenty-Third. The Psalmist experienced both. Even Jesus experienced both. Crests and troughs. Mountains and valleys. Highs and lows. Faithfulness and abandonment. Trust and doubt. The waters gush forth, fresh and cold then the well runs dry.

For most of us faith is easy up on the mountains when life is good and going our way. But, for most of us, faith is tough down in the valley, when life is hard, and the well runs dry. So, enjoy the mountains when you're there. Endure the valleys. For as surely as morning follows night, as surely as spring follows winter, as surely as the sun follows the rains the crests and peaks will come again for those who keep the faith and endure to the end.

Notes, Insights, Reflections

Endnotes

[i] All Scripture references are from the New Revised Standard Version of the Bible.

[ii] Augustine, *Confessions*, trans. Henry Chadwick, (New York: Oxford University Press, Inc., 2008), 3.

[iii] Tom Brown, *The Tracker: The True Story of Tom Brown, Jr.,* (New York: Berkley Books, 1986).

[iv] Tom Brown, *The Tracker: The True Story of Tom Brown, Jr.*